Substack Mastery: Insider Secrets from a Content Strategist & Seasoned Author

Learn the Basics, Stay Motivated, Grow Your Paid Subscribers, & Thrive with a Community.

Dr Mehmet Yildiz

Leader of ILLUMINATION Community on Substack & Medium

Substack Mastery

Dr Mehmet Yildiz

Published by Mehmet Yildiz, 2024.

Table of Contents

First Edition, September 2024
Copyright © Dr Mehmet Yildiz
Publisher: S.T.E.P.S. Publishing Australia
P.O Box 2097, Roxburgh Park, Victoria, 3064 Australia
Edited by Mark Longfield, Dr Michael Broadly, Dr Albert Jones

<u>Disclaimer</u>

Table of Contents

1. Foundation and Mindset
2. Building Trust and Engagement
3. Growth and Adaptability
4. Strategy and Planning
5. Monetization and Scaling
6. Tools and Optimization
7. Content Creation and Delivery
8. Reader Experience and Interaction
9. Inspiration and Growth Mindset

Introduction: Why I Wrote This Book

A few months ago, when I publicly announced that I would dedicate **80% of my time to Substack, 15% to Newsbreak, and just 5% to Medium**[1], I received an intriguing call from one of my book publishers. This serendipitous encounter was inspiring, much like **one of my stories that also brought serendipity**[2]. Whenever **serendipity knocks on my door**[3], I answer graciously.

The company's CEO, who also happens to be a close friend, told me they were looking for a seasoned writer to write about Substack as a trendy topic in the publishing world. With my background and proven track record of publishing best-selling books, she said I was the best candidate for the job. So she approached me first.

She asked if I would be interested. I said yes, but I was clear that I didn't want to pursue traditional publishing as we had in the past. Understanding my need for freedom, she offered a hybrid publishing model that nicely suited my needs.

However, she emphasized that the market on this topic was growing rapidly, and they wanted the book to be marketed to their clients within a month, so she requested the book proposal within three days. I agreed and sent the proposal with a table of contents. Within a day, they approved it with some additional suggestions.

---

1. https://medium.com/illumination/why-my-wise-mentors-advised-me-80-substack-15-newsbreak-5-medium-for-my-writing-effort-e1bf33b4e4b7

2. https://medium.com/illumination/an-unexpected-55k-contract-a-new-client-and-a-soulmate-were-born-out-of-a-simple-story-on-medium-b51af71058a3

3. https://medium.com/sensible-biohacking-transhumanism/heres-how-serendipity-and-karma-positively-affected-the-quality-of-my-life-afc5a81ee89a

The key point was that the book needed to be written in an autobiographical format, filled with hands-on experience and evidence-based claims, not just theoretical or motivational content. There are already plenty of such books, and they don't sell well.

As you may know, publishers are focused on the bottom line, and even though she is my friend, she had to ensure the company's financial success in this economic climate.

They then gave me one month to complete the first draft for approval. Compared to my technical and scientific books, this was a breeze to write.

After work and **daily meditation**[4], I simply talked to myself in **a flow state**[5], turned those self-conversations into text, and, with minor self-editing, sent it to a proofreader sponsored by the publishing company. This week, I submitted the manuscript, which will now undergo professional editing.

I have set up preorders for both the digital and paperback versions of **my book on Amazon**[6] and will soon make my editions available through my syndicated publishing company, which offers a lower commission.

The traditional publishing company will manage its own sales in global markets, but based on my past experience, the commission I receive from them is minimal—essentially pocket money. That's why I've moved away from exclusive traditional publishing, as **I explained in a previous story a few years ago.**[7]

Preface: Why I Wrote This Book About Substack for New Readers

WELCOME TO AN EXCITING virtual journey that could transform your approach to digital content creation, marketing, distribution, and sales. I will introduce a simple yet very powerful tool: Substack.

---

4.   https://medium.com/p/34c85c6bfac6

5.   https://medium.com/sensible-biohacking-transhumanism/5-tips-to-enter-a-flow-state-and-improve-work-joy-and-health-d4850166bb22

6.   https://www.amazon.com/dp/B0DF2K6VNX

7.   https://medium.com/illumination-book-chapters/the-joy-of-selling-1-000-books-in-a-month-with-minimal-investment-13a24a6354c1

Imagine diving into the vast ocean of online writing as a freelancer, only to find yourself lost in the waves of noise and competition, causing stress and anxiety.

Finding your voice, growing your audience, and building a sustainable newsletter can feel like solving a complex puzzle. But what if you had a clear map to guide you through this labyrinth? That's exactly what I have aimed to provide with this new book.

For the past five years, I have been deeply immersed in the Substack ecosystem, weaving together my 42+ years of experience in content development, strategy, and marketing with a background as a scientist, technologist, inventor, and community leader.

This book is the product of this journey, with its ups and downs, written in an autobiographical style. It is a practical, heartfelt guide designed to help freelance writers and content entrepreneurs discover and amplify their unique voices, grow their audiences, earn income from their creations, and build a sustainable newsletter-based content development and marketing business.

As a new reader, you might be asking, "Why should I invest my precious time in another book about writing?" The answer is simple and personal.

Throughout my career as a now semi-retired technology/science consultant for large organizations and startup companies, I have witnessed countless talented people struggle with the same challenges freelance writers face.

Finding their footing in the world of digital content creation and audience building is a daunting task. As a person with high **digital intelligence**[8], strong emotional intelligence, an admirable **adversity quotient**[9], and a reasonable IQ, I struggled and even failed multiple times with strong fallback positions. Those who don't have sufficient levels of these types of intelligence are prone to a more painful failure even before they start.

I witnessed that despite the flashy success stories and grand promises, there has often been a missing piece in the publishing industry: real, hands-on guidance that addresses the everyday struggles of content creators. My new book is my way of bridging that gap.

---

8.   https://medium.com/technology-hits/summary-of-digital-intelligence-db6303f4f3de

9.   https://medium.com/sensible-biohacking-transhumanism/how-i-increased-my-aq-to-leave-a-more-peaceful-and-enjoyable-life-1bfc0c646034

Although I come from an academic background and know the importance of solid theory behind practice, my new book is not just about theory or abstract concepts.

I offer my struggles honestly and humbly, my true feelings, my triumphs, and failures with practical and actionable insights born from my own experience of growing a Substack to **around 30,000 subscribers**[10], my publications to 100,000+ subscribers, and earning the endorsement of 491 fellow Substack writers without even promoting my services. They helped me gain 4,000 subscribers. This shows the importance of endorsements for Substack Writers as the first lesson.

I HAVE WALKED THE PATH you are on now. Therefore, I want to share the lessons I have learned — triumphs and trials — with you.

As you turn the digital or paperback pages of my new book, here's what you will be surprised by and what you will uncover as unspoken truth:

- You will discover how to unearth and develop your unique perspective, making your content stand out and deeply connect with your readers.
- You will learn proven strategies for attracting and retaining readers, from crafting captivating content to effective promotion techniques that work.
- You will gain insights into creating a content ecosystem that supports long-term growth and engagement, ensuring your newsletters or platforms remain vibrant and relevant.
- You will get practical guidance on transforming your Substack newsletters into a viable income source tailored to your current growth stage.
- Last but not least, you will find real-world solutions to common obstacles faced by content creators like freelancers or content

---

10.   https://substack.com/@drmehmetyildiz

entrepreneurs, including maintaining consistency and managing reader requirements and expectations.

- As a bonus, I will give an opportunity to the readers of my book to be part of my diverse and supportive community and vast network.

My initial consultant editors posed the question, as usual: "What sets this book apart?"

I told them this wasn't another book filled with flashy promises or theoretical fluff. This is a grounded, hands-on guide distilled from years of practical experience in simple language anyone can understand.

I designed it to serve as a tool that freelance writers or content entrepreneurs can use immediately, offering actionable strategies and real-world guidance and tips in a constructive and realistic way.

This book isn't about quick fixes or passing fads. It covers insights into building a sustainable legacy of professional growth and personal fulfilmentthrough captivating, meaningful, impactful, helpful, memorable, inspiring, and nuanced content creation.

I am excited to start this journey with my fellow writers and editors. By the end of this book, you will have the knowledge and confidence to grow your audience, build thriving Substack newsletters, and make your mark in the world of content creation and distribution.

Thank you for joining my journey. Let's start the learning process with meaningful engagement for mutual benefit. Together, we can navigate this content labyrinth and build something truly extraordinary.

I look forward to your feedback as a beta reader. I will publish this on multiple platforms for free to give my beta readers the opportunity to refine it and make it a valuable knowledge source and illuminating reference for society.

The funds generated from this book will be donated to the management of **the Substack Mastery site for the ILLUMINATION community.**[11] This education site also amplifies the newsletters of freelance writers.

The book has links to some of my articles related to writing on Medium for interested readers to discover my stories and learn about my community. If you are not interested in joining Medium, you can skip those links.

---

11.   https://illuminationcurators.substack.com/

Chapter 1: What is Substack, why it matters, and how to start it

As an avid reader, I am captivated by the preface and first chapter of any book. If it grabs my attention, I keep reading it.

In a nutshell, this book is the product of my Substack journey, with its ups and downs, written in an autobiographical style. It is a practical, heartfelt guide designed to help freelance writers and content entrepreneurs discover and amplify their unique voices, grow their audiences, earn income from their creations, and build a sustainable newsletter-based content development and marketing business.

Welcome to Chapter 1 of Substack Mastery. I wrote this chapter for absolute beginners. If you already have an account and created a newsletter, you can quickly skim through and read the key takeaways.

What is Substack, why it matters, and how to start it

Substack is a digital platform that allows writers to publish newsletters directly to their audience. It combines elements of blogging, article writing, storytelling, and sending email newsletters.

The platform provides writers with tools to monetize their content through subscriptions and providing links to services or products. Substack is flexible as writers can offer both free and paid content. When writers monetize their content, Substack takes 10% of the subscription income, so 90% of the income goes to writers.

As highlighted in my latest story[1], Substack has consistently demonstrated a deep commitment to nurturing creators at all levels, from absolute beginners

---

1. https://medium.com/illumination/why-my-wise-mentors-advised-me-80-substack-15-newsbreak-5-medium-for-my-writing-effort-e1bf33b4e4b7

to established writers and even celebrities. Substack's dedication to creator support is unmatched. It has a proven track record of creating success across diverse content genres. Therefore, the platform grows rapidly.

Substack started in 2017, but it grew so fast that it now hosts millions of newsletters across various genres. According to this resource[2], Substack gets over 20 million monthly active subscribers and has reached 2 million paid subscriptions.

With more than 17,000 writers earning income through the platform, the top 10 authors collectively make **$25 million** annually. One of my mentors, who urged me to stop and start with Substack, earns $100K monthly via Substack newsletters. He used to earn around 1K on Medium.com, where he has many more followers than me.

Substack's user base continues to expand globally, offering a broad audience for writers. The platform has attracted well-known authors, journalists, and professionals from different disciplines, contributing to its widespread recognition and influence.

From my experience, two new technical features helped Substack gain a lot of traction. The first one is the improved algorithm for distributing posts across the platform without censorship. The second one is their embedded social media tool, Substack Notes. The tool is easy to use and has multiple functions to build an audience around our work. In addition, the platform has an AI-assisted intelligent Helpdesk for creators.

Thanks to these technological additions and the platform's diligent and caring focus on creators, Substack became a premier platform for content creators, solidifying its position as the #1 choice for effective and impactful content distribution worldwide.

Section 2: Why to Start Substack Now?

First and foremost, if you are a writer on Medium or any other platform, you don't need to leave them to start on Substack. Far from it, using the power of those platforms, you can even be more successful on Substack. If someone tries to convince you to leave these platforms think about it logically and verify the source and motives.

---

2.   https://backlinko.com/substack-users

In this book or my articles, I don't tell my readers what they should do; instead, I share my experiences and observations. I started Substack based on the recommendation of an entrepreneurial friend who sold over a million books through her mailing list, which is managed by Substack without a paid subscription.

This unusual approach did not convince me as I did not like the idea of moving my hard-earned and regularly cleaned mailing list. I still don't do it and use my own list on my own platform. I created an account and started adding a few important posts for organic viewing. My goal was not sales but to build a community.

During that period, within the last five years, I invested 99% of my writing efforts in Medium, as it appealed to me more than Substack, where I couldn't find any engagement or community spirit. However, in 2023, Medium significantly changed its rules and algorithm, so the visibility of my stories and the engagement rate substantially declined.

This setback inspired me to reconsider Substack. Although I gained a few thousand free subscribers in the last five years, the real spike happened after turning on the monetization options and several loyal readers supporting my newsletters as paid clients.

This minor decision made a massive impact as Substack started promoting my content to my audience and the new one through its website, application (app), and social media platform (Notes). Within a few months, I gained an extra 20,000 subscribers. Some of them even became paid subscribers.

When my proteges asked why they should start Substack in addition to Medium, I shared my personal experience and observations on the platform. I will summarize the key points. They now understand that starting a Substack can be a game-changer for creators, freelance writers, entrepreneurs, and professionals. Readers now want curated and valuable content from established writers.

As a freelancer writer, the most important reason is a direct connection with your audience. Substack allows creators to build a direct relationship with their readers. It has no middlemen and no algorithms deciding who sees your content if you have subscribers. But if you don't have subscribers, the algorithm has multiple functions to bring free subscribers and even tries to make them pay subscribers by creating visibility and prompting them.

The second compelling reason is an opportunity to monetize content, especially if you have expertise in a specific area. Creators and professionals can turn their knowledge and skills into income. Substack offers tools to set up paid subscriptions, letting them earn from the content they produce. It is an easy and practical way to monetize our expertise and passion.

From my perspective, unlike social media platforms, where we are at the mercy of changing algorithms, Substack gives us ownership of our content and subscriber list. We can add or subtract. This control means we can grow and engage our audience on our terms. Substack does not tell us what to do. Instead, it helps us to support our audience better by being on our side as creators and professionals.

I found Substack easy to use. It has a user-friendly interface. It is flexible and offers a simple configuration. You don't need to be tech-savvy to start. Setting up your account and newsletter is straightforward, so you can focus more on creating content rather than dealing with complicated tech. I will cover the details in the next section.

For me, the most important aspect was **building a community around my work.** By sharing our insights in articles or stories, it is possible to create a community around our content. Engaging directly with our subscribers helps us build a loyal audience who values our perspectives and experiences.

In this information age, readers are metaphorically flooded with information, and they don't know how to drink from a firehose. Therefore, with so much content, having a dedicated space where people can regularly engage with our work helps us stand out. I see this as a great opportunity to carve out our own niche and establish our voice.

In short, positioning yourself for success in a rapidly growing and supportive space offers personal and professional growth opportunities. I will discuss details in the next chapters of this book.

Starting your Substack is an exciting way to connect with readers and share your unique voice. Throughout this book, I will provide a detailed roadmap to help you launch and grow your newsletter. Now, let me get you started with the basics.

Section 3: How to Start Substack?

First, go to Substack's website[3] and click on the sign-in button at the top right of the screen.

Then click on the Create an account button, as shown in the following screen capture.

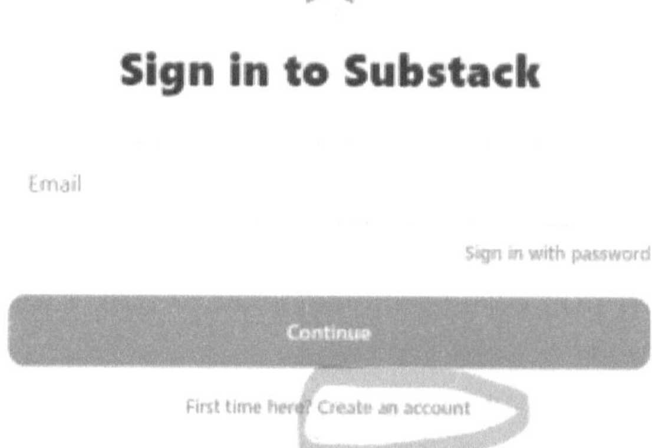

It prompts you to choose some topics you might be interested in reading and writing. You choose the relevant ones.

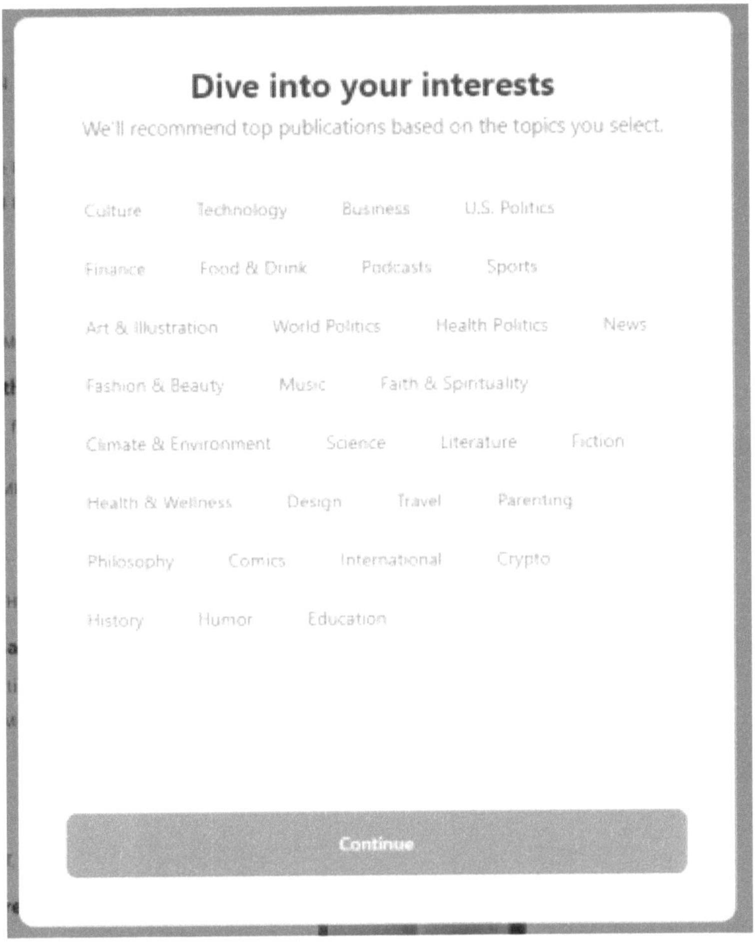

Dive into your interests

We'll recommend top publications based on the topics you select.

Culture   Technology   Business   U.S. Politics

Finance   Food & Drink   Podcasts   Sports

Art & Illustration   World Politics   Health Politics   News

Fashion & Beauty   Music   Faith & Spirituality

Climate & Environment   Science   Literature   Fiction

Health & Wellness   Design   Travel   Parenting

Philosophy   Comics   International   Crypto

History   Humor   Education

Continue

Then, it prompts you to seven popular newsletters. You may select or unselect them as shown below.

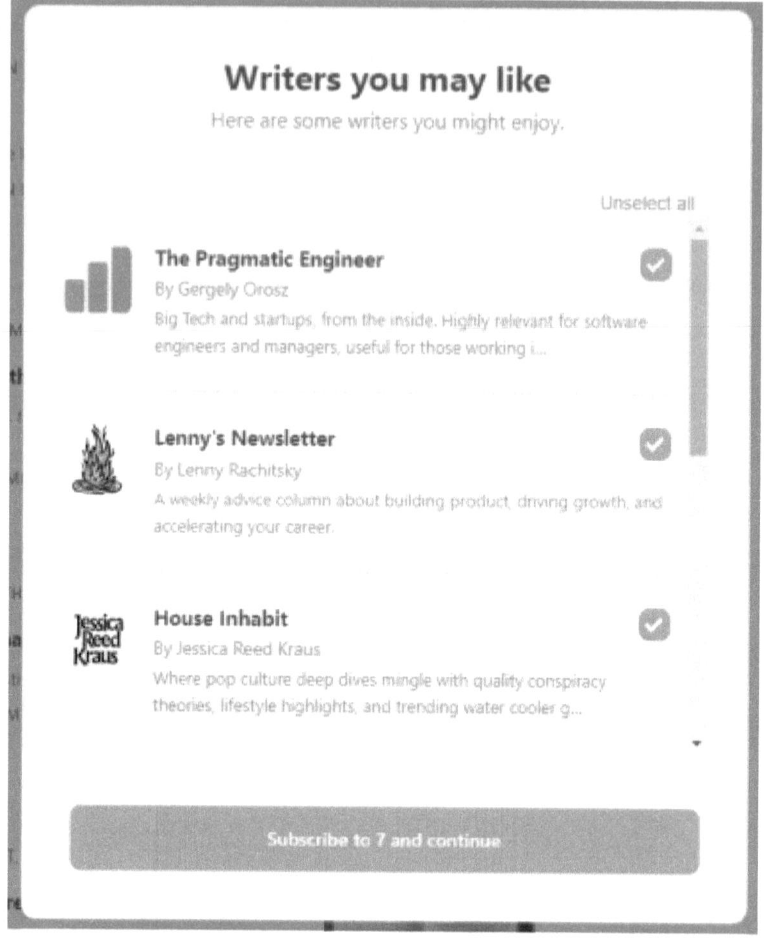

Then, you will be prompted to create an account. This requires a valid email address, as shown below.

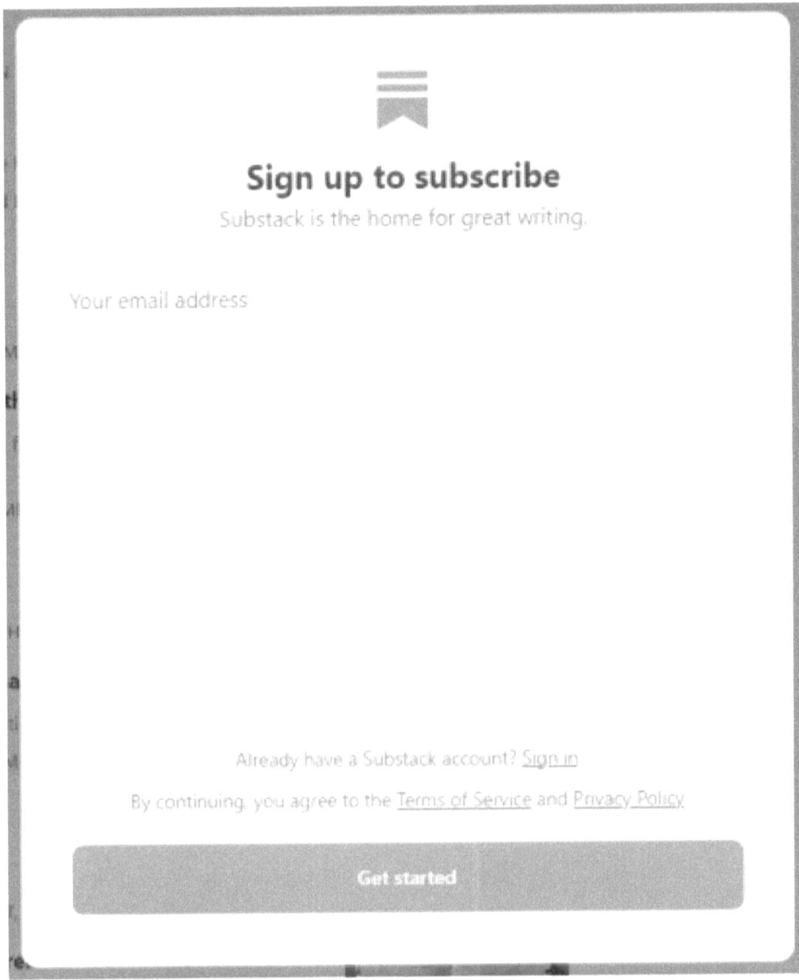

You fill in the following three boxes. You can change them later.

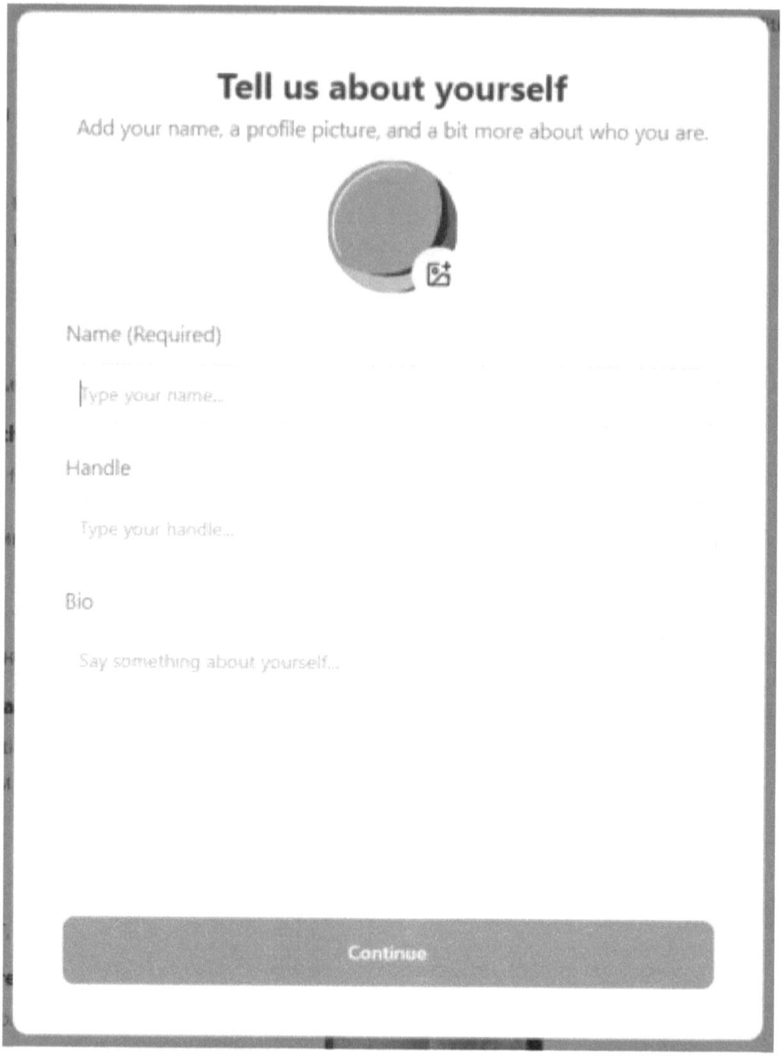

Tell us about yourself

Add your name, a profile picture, and a bit more about who you are.

Name (Required)

Type your name...

Handle

Type your handle...

Bio

Say something about yourself...

Continue

You can download the application if you wish. After that, you will be informed that you can start reading.

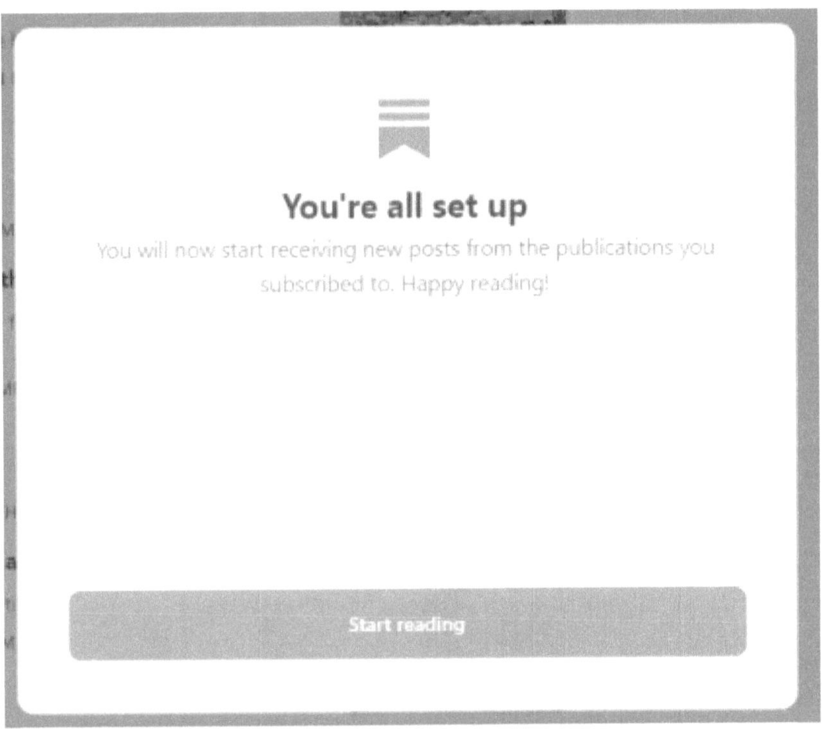

How about writing?

AS A WRITER, YOU NEED to create a publication. To do that you click on the "Create your Substack" button as shown below.

It is a good idea to choose a memorable publication name and URL that reflects your brand or niche. Some people just use their name like John's Substack, but this is not a good idea as imagine how many people there are with that name. The likelihood of a reader subscribing to such a name is very low. I keep highlighting this undermined yet critical point.

You also need to write a concise overview of your newsletter's focus and what readers can expect. This is your elevator pitch to attract subscribers.

It is a good idea to upload a professional profile picture and a captivating cover photo that aligns with your content and target audience.

Decide whether to offer free, paid, or both subscription tiers. If you choose paid, set a pricing structure that reflects the value you provide.

It is important to welcome your readers. So you need to design a welcoming subscription page with a clear call to action and a preview of the benefits subscribers will receive. Create a consistent publication schedule (e.g., weekly, bi-weekly, or monthly) to keep your audience engaged and anticipating your content.

To write your first story, you can click on the Start publishing button.

It will open the Substack editor to write your first post. You can use formatting tools to structure your content, add visuals, and include links for further exploration. However, before hitting the "Publish" button it is a good idea to preview your post to ensure it looks and reads exactly as you intend.

After publishing your story, remember to share your post on social media, including Facebook, X, Instagram, and LinkedIn. However, the most important one is "Share as a note" because this is where you build your community by interacting with your readers and other writers.

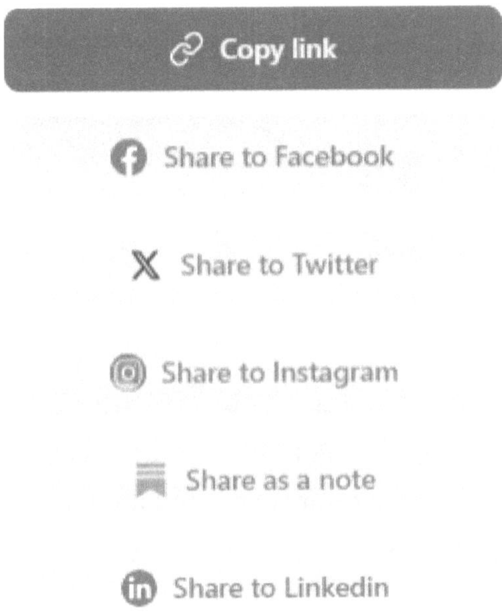

IT IS IMPORTANT TO share your post across multiple social media platforms to reach a wider audience. However, it is also important to engage with other writers and readers within the Substack community and relevant online spaces.

You may also expand your reach by contributing guest posts to other blogs or newsletters with a similar audience. You may invite comments and feedback on your posts and actively respond to build a community.

While supporting all subscribers, it is important to offer special content or benefits to paid subscribers to encourage loyalty and increase conversions.

Data is important to understand your progress. So, it is a good idea to use Substack's analytics to understand your audience's preferences and tailor your content accordingly. Here is what the stats page looks like:

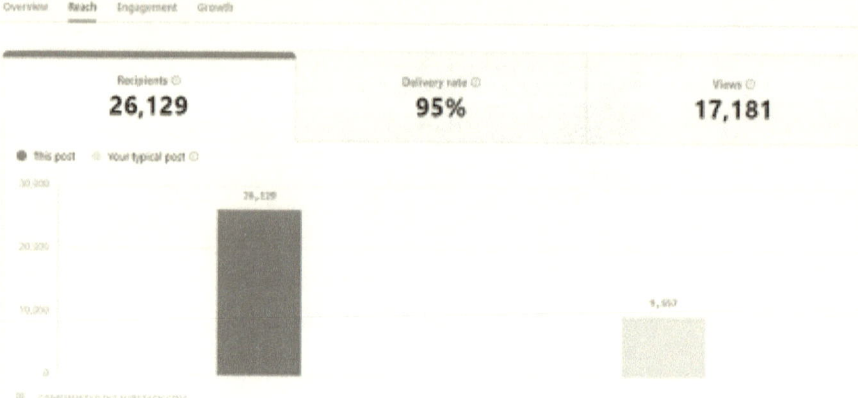

It provides an overview and shows the reach, engagement, and growth of each post. You may also check publication statistic (stats), which give valuable information on the performance of your publication. Here is a sample screen capture of one of my publications related to health.[4]

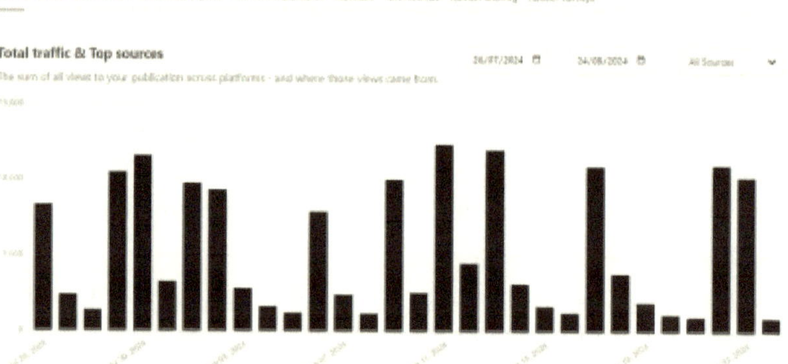

The fluctuations usually indicate the days I sent emails and the traffic coming from the Substack app or website. The good news is that my publication gets some traffic even if I don't post and send emails. I will cover the interpretation of stats in another chapter in detail.

From my experience running three specialized newsletters, premium content is critical to monetizing your content. So, you may try to attract paid subscribers by offering exclusive, high-value content like in-depth analysis, interviews, or early access to new work.

---

4.   https://dryildiz.substack.com/

Once you have established a substantial following, you may explore partnerships with sponsors or even consider relevant advertisements that might match your content and newsletter theme.

Please also remember to collaborate with other freelancer writers and content entrepreneurs. By engaging in their content, you can build good relationships, and they can even endorse your newsletters. For example, I gained **3000 subscribers from 456 Substack writers** who recommended my Content Strategy, Development, & Marketing Insights[5] newsletter.

Conclusions and Key Takeaways

The most important takeaway is being patient and consistent. Building a successful Substack newsletter and audience takes time and dedication.

We must focus on creating high-quality content, nurturing our readers and community, and experimenting with different strategies to find what works best.

With persistence and passion, your newsletter can grow and thrive for your writing and be a valuable resource for your readers. Substack offers a powerful platform for writers to share their work and build a dedicated audience.

By following these basic steps, you can start your own newsletter, engage with your readers, and potentially monetize your content. The key is to remain consistent, provide valuable content, and actively engage with your community.

As we grow and evolve, exploring new horizons is crucial. Substack emerges as a powerful ally in this journey, offering unmatched support and a robust system to help us on our content and audience effectively.

If you are a writer on Medium, you have an additional advantage in building and growing your audience faster. Medium and Substack each have unique strengths that, when leveraged together, can propel you to new heights in your writing career.

Substack's flexibility and comprehensive support make it an ideal companion to Medium. It ensures that you are not confined to a single platform but can expand your influence and engage with a broader audience.

If you are uncomfortable with Substack initially and you feel you are making no progress, please don't give up. It is normal. I will provide practical and valuable tips in the next chapters with a helpful checklist.

---

5.   https://drmehmetyildiz.substack.com/

Chapter 2: What is Substack Notes, why does it matter for freelance writers, and how do you start it in 5 minutes and use it to build an audience efficiently?

What caught their attention about Substack Notes?

I mentioned the Substack Notes **in the previous chapter** [1]as the key to unlocking audience growth and boosting paid subscriptions via the Substack.com website and its excellent application.

When I revealed that **80% of Substack's success hinges on the proper and effective use of Notes,** suddenly, everyone was listening. They were eager to know more, craving the details on how to use this powerful tool.

I told them, "You'll find out in the next chapter." Substack Notes are not just important — they are essential for success. That's exactly why this second chapter of my book will dive deep into mastering Notes, the strategy that could transform your Substack journey. Stay tuned because this is where the real magic happens.

When I first started using Substack Notes on 11 April 2023 after reading **an educational and inspiring post** [2] by **Chris Best** [3], **Hamish McKenzie** [4], and

1. https://medium.com/illumination/substack-mastery-book-chapter-1-cb3104341985

2.   https://on.substack.com/p/introducing-notes

3.   https://substack.com/@cb

4.   https://substack.com/@hamish

Jairaj Sethi[5], co-founders of Substack, I quickly realized how powerful this tool could be for growing my audience, increasing paid subscribers, and establishing myself as a content strategist.

If you are a creator, freelance writer, solopreneur, content entrepreneur, or content marketing strategist like me, you will want to know how to make the most of Substack Notes to take your newsletter to the next level. In this chapter, I will explain how I have been using Substack Notes and how you can too.

A Brief Introduction to My Tutorials for My Proteges

MY PROTEGES ASKED ME how they could grow their Substack audience with Notes. My answer was that one of the best things about Substack Notes is that it lets you connect with your audience in a more casual, bite-sized way.

I have found that sharing quick thoughts, ideas, or sneak peeks of upcoming newsletters keeps my readers engaged and curious. It's like giving them a small appetizer before the main course, which makes them more likely to subscribe for the full meal.

Then, they asked me about Substack newsletter marketing tips. Marketing a newsletter can be challenging, but Notes has made it much easier for me.

I use Notes to share highlights from my newsletters or behind-the-scenes stories that give readers a glimpse into my writing process. This keeps my current subscribers engaged and attracts new readers intrigued by my offer.

My focus was on boosting Substack's subscriber count. I have noticed that it drives up my subscriber count when I use Notes to create a sense of urgency or exclusivity — like announcing a special edition or offering limited-time content.

People love feeling like they are getting something special, and Notes is the ideal place to tease those exclusive benefits.

The subscribers of my **Content Strategy, Development, & Marketing Insights**[6] asked me about effective substack promotion strategies. I told them that collaborating with other writers has been a game-changer for me. To this end Substack, Notes is a fantastic tool for this.

---

5.   https://substack.com/@jairaj

6.   https://drmehmetyildiz.substack.com/

By featuring other writers in my Notes and asking them to do the same for me, I have been able to tap into new audiences and grow my reach. It is all about building a community and supporting each other's growth.

Another common question was how to increase newsletter engagement on Substack. I have known for a long time that engagement is key to building a loyal audience on any platform.

So, Substack Notes is a great way to keep the conversation going. I like to use Notes to ask questions, start discussions or invite feedback on my latest newsletter. This kind of interaction keeps my readers engaged and encourages them to share my content with others.

Some proteges asked about the possibility of monetizing their Substack newsletter. I have found that using Notes to share previews or insights from my premium content is a subtle yet effective way to convert free subscribers into paid ones. I usually highlight how others have benefited from my paid content, which helps persuade those on the fence to take the plunge.

My focus is on best practices for Substack growth. Consistency is crucial to achieving this goal. I have made it a habit to regularly post on Notes, but I always focus on quality over quantity. Each post needs to add value and be relevant to my audience. This consistency has helped me maintain steady growth and keep my readers returning for more.

Many freelance writers with whom I interact usually ask me to give them Substack success tips for creators. I told them experimentation is your friend. When I first started using Notes, I tried different types of content — short thoughts, recommendations, polls — to see what resonated best with my audience. By tracking what drives the most traffic and subscriptions, I've been able to refine my strategy and focus on what works.

A key point is optimizing Substack for maximum reach. I have found that optimizing my Notes with relevant keywords has made a big difference. I used phrases my audience might be searching for, like "Grow Your Substack Audience" or "Effective Substack Promotion Strategies." This helps my Notes appear in searches, attracting new readers and expanding my reach.

Some content entrepreneurs, founding members of my **Content Strategy, Development, & Marketing Insights**[7], asked about Substack content strategy for creators, curators, editors, and content marketers.

---

7.   https://drmehmetyildiz.substack.com/

I responded that I have integrated Substack Notes into my overall content strategy. I use my Notes alongside my newsletters, ensuring they complement each other and align with my goals.

Whether we are building anticipation for an upcoming newsletter or continuing the conversation afterwards, Using Substack Notes is crucial in keeping my audience engaged and informed.

So, I can highlight that Substack Notes has truly been a game-changer for me as a content strategist and writer. Using it strategically allows us to grow our audience, increase engagement, and monetize our content more effectively. I hope these insights inspire you to make the most of this powerful tool and take your Substack to new heights.

Substack Notes is a quick and easy way to connect with your audience, share ideas, and promote your newsletter. It's perfect for staying in touch with your readers without the pressure of writing a full newsletter each time.

How to Get Started with Substack Notes: A Simple Guide for Beginners

IF YOU ARE NEW TO SUBSTACK Notes, don't worry — it is easy to get started. Substack Notes is a great way to share quick updates and thoughts and engage with your audience in a more casual way. Here's a step-by-step guide to help you begin:

Step 1: Access Substack Notes

LOG IN TO SUBSTACK: Start by logging into your Substack account. If you don't have one yet, you will need to sign up at **Substack.com**[8]. Please check out **Chapter 1 of my Substack Mastery book**[9] for details.

Find Notes: Once you are logged in, go to your Substack account. You will see an icon for "Notes" on the left-hand side menu. Click on it to enter the Notes section. I illustrated it in the following screenshot.

---

8. https://substack.com

9. https://medium.com/illumination/substack-mastery-book-chapter-1-cb3104341985

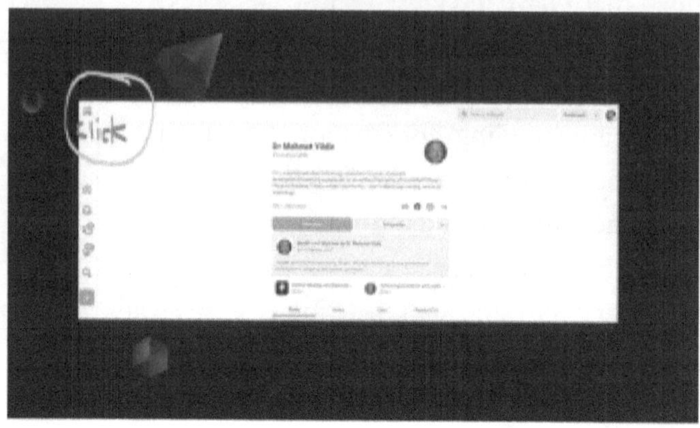

Step 2: Create Your First Note

YOU WILL SEE THE FOLLOWING message box.

You type some text, and you will see two options. You can either send it to everyone or only your paid subscribers. After finishing your note, just post it.

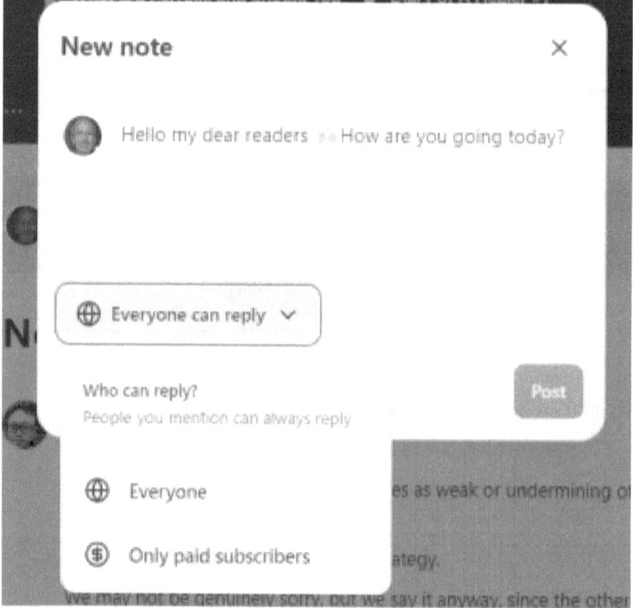

Please remember that Notes are meant to be short and sweet, so think of it as writing a quick post or update. You can share a thought, a link, or a preview of your next newsletter. To make your Note more engaging, you can add links or images by using the toolbar above the text box.

When happy with your Note, click the "Publish" button. Your Note will now be shared with subscribers and anyone following you on Substack.

After publishing, readers might respond to your Note. This is a great way to start conversations and connect with your audience with four interaction options.

Here is an inspiring post from one of my favourite authors, **Jerry Keszka**[10], which I **liked**, **restacked**, **commented** on, and **shared** in my circles.

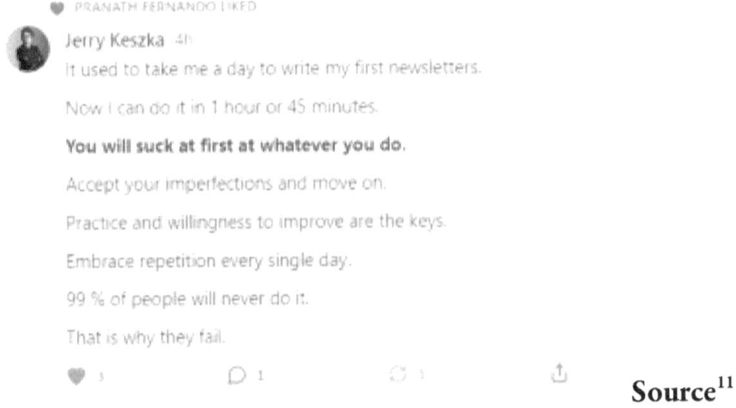

Source[11]

I Interviewed Jerry today so you can learn about his background.

Interview with Jerry Keszka, PhD[12]

A scientist, businessman, and accomplished writer[13]

Let me explain how you can engage in a note like this. The first icon at the bottom of the note is to like it. The second is to leave a comment. The third is to restack, which shows on your profile, and the third icon is for sharing the note on your socials. The entire interaction takes only one minute.

---

10.   https://medium.com/u/31a29ac4804

11.   https://substack.com/@jerrykeszka/note/c-66641958

12.   https://medium.com/illumination/interview-with-jerry-keszka-phd-848d37a87817

13.   https://medium.com/illumination/interview-with-jerry-keszka-phd-848d37a87817

Here is a professional note posted by **Sylvain Zyssman**[14] who is a wonderful collaborator whom **I interviewed and introduced to my audience.**[15] This note shows how you can collaborate with others.

Source[16]

I also interviewed Sylvain so you can learn about his background.

<u>Interview with Sylvain Zyssman</u>[17]

<u>CTO | Data Scientist | Strategist | Mentor | Writer | Speaker</u>[18]

---

14.   https://medium.com/u/b95c494f06a

15.   https://medium.com/illumination/interview-with-sylvain-zyssman-d4e748baf326

16.   https://substack.com/@sylzys/note/c-66468348

17.   https://medium.com/illumination/interview-with-sylvain-zyssman-d4e748baf326

18.   https://medium.com/illumination/interview-with-sylvain-zyssman-d4e748baf326

Step 3: Explore Notes from Others

YOU CAN SEE WHAT OTHER writers are sharing on Substack Notes. Go back to the Notes section and scroll through posts from people you follow. This can give you inspiration for your own Notes.

If you find a Note you like, feel free to "like" it or leave a comment. Engaging with other writers can help you grow your network and learn from others.

Step 4: Use Notes to Grow Your Audience

THE MORE YOU SHARE, the more your audience will stay engaged. Try to post Notes regularly to keep your subscribers interested. Use Notes to highlight your newsletter. Share snippets or teasers that make readers want to check out the full content.

Step 5: Use Notes to Chat with Your Loyal Readers Privately

YOU CAN ALSO USE NOTES for private chat and build your relationships. It is easy and enjoyable. You need to find the profile of the author/reader and click on the Message button as shown below.

Practical Tips for Beginners

KEEP IT SIMPLE: Notes don't have to be long or complicated. Just share what's on your mind!

Be Consistent: Try to post Notes consistently to keep your audience engaged.

Interact: Engage with other writers and readers by commenting and liking their Substack Notes.

That's it! With these simple steps, you're ready to start using Substack Notes. Happy writing, reading, engaging, and sharing!

Chapter 3: How to Grow on Substack with Peer Recommendations and Powerful Sharing Tools

Welcome to chapter three of Substack Mastery Book ◈

Section 1: The Importance of Restacking and How to Do It

There are so many sharing features on Substack that I could have written an entire book about it. But I don't want to overwhelm my readers, so I distilled the most important ones into a short section.

One of the easiest ways to share Substack posts is restacking them. I restack every Substack post I read daily for good reasons. Restacking allows us to reshare posts from other Substack writers within our own publication, similar to retweeting on X or reposting on LinkedIn. It helps nurture the community and highlights content we find valuable, which can attract like-minded readers.

Every Substack post comes with the Restack option underneath.

For example, earlier, **Warren Brown**[1] restacked a post of **Alina Pitt**[2]. As I follow this great writer both on Medium and now on Substack, their restacks show on my Substack notes.

---

1.   https://medium.com/u/a30745e0996d

2.   https://medium.com/u/66eeaa985fff

Now, to amplify Alina's post, I click on the restack button, which gives me two options, as shown in the screenshot below.

When I click on the Restack with a note, I get an opportunity to leave a brief note like the following. I ensure everyone sees my reply and finds a chance to find Alina's great story and connect with Alina and Warren through this message. As I have over 29K subscribers on Substack, this simple note can significantly increase the chance of visibility of these two great writers via the Substack Notes.

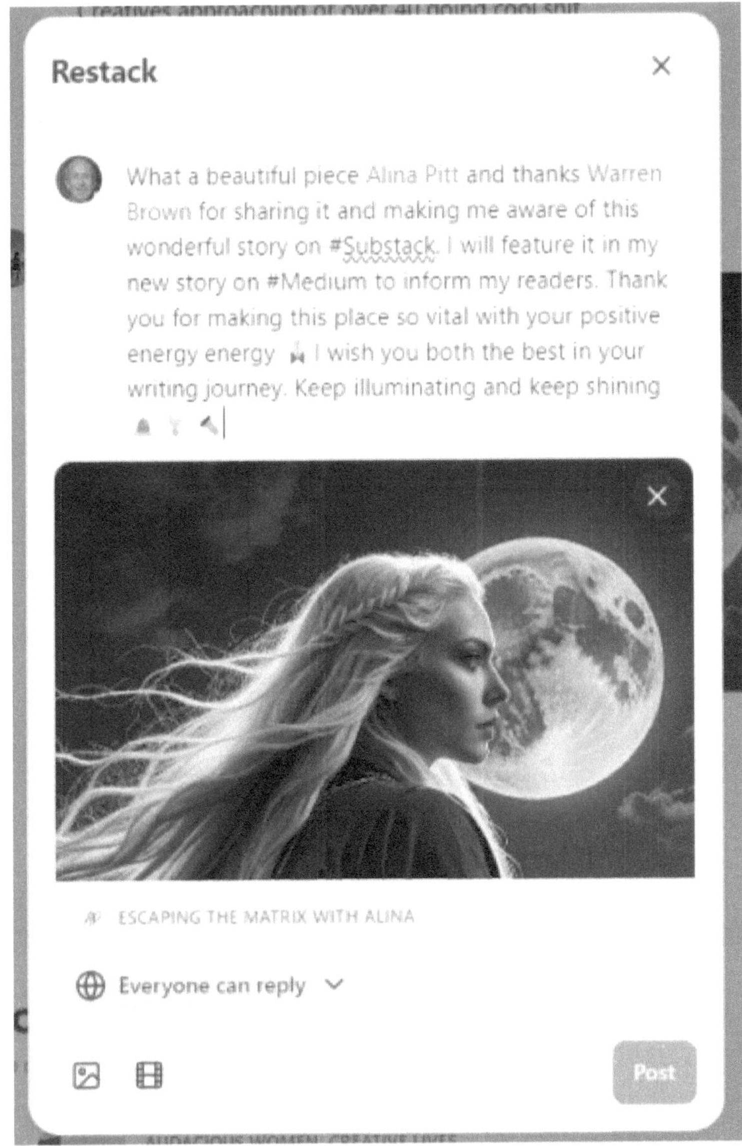

When you finish your note, just click on the Post button at the bottom right side of the window. That's it. It is now distributed by the unbiased algorithm of the Substack ecosystem. Unlike other social media platforms, there are no biased curators who can censor your post. The Substack algorithm is the opposite of the Medium algorithm and shows it to all your subscribers via Notes.

Apart from the amplification through the magical Substack Notes, wow, the best part is Alina's article posted by Warren shows on my Substack profile available to my 29K subscribers who might be curious about what I found, read, and shared today as shown in the following screen capture.

Dr Mehmet Yildiz

@drmehmetyildiz

I'm a scientist/executive technology consultant (42 years of content development/marketing experience). As an author/chief editor of ILLUMINATION on Medium/Substack, I lead a writers' community. I own 3 newsletters: writing, health, & technology

29K+ subscribers

   +4

New post Edit profile ...

Health and Wellness by Dr Mehmet Yildiz
By Dr Mehmet Yildiz

Articles about health, well-being, fitness, self-improvement, personal/professional development, longevity and disease prevention

 Content Strategy, Development ...
Writer

 Technology Excellence and Leade ...
Writer

Posts   Notes   Likes   Reads (189)

 Dr Mehmet Yildiz · 5m ...

What a beautiful piece Alina Pitt and thanks Warren Brown for sharing it and making me aware of this wonderful story on #Substack. I will feature it in my new story on #Medium to inform my readers. Thank you for making this place so vital with your positive energy energy ✨ I wish you both the best in your writing journey. Keep illuminating and keep shining ✨

Feeling The Super Blue Moon

What to Expect - August 2024

Now, my subscribers can like, comment, restack, and share Alina's posts. Imagine 1,000 readers engaging with it! Substack Notes then shows the post to all of those subscribers, creating a powerful ripple effect.

This is one of Substack's most impactful features, making sharing and connecting so easy. I wish Medium would take note and implement such creator-focused features instead of low-impact ones.

The key takeaway: Add a comment or note, tag relevant writers, and use these sharing features to maximize your reach and grow your Substack audience.

Section 2: Grow Your Substack Audience with Recommendations

The Substack Recommendations feature was **introduced on 12 April 2022**[3]. It excited me because it looked very promising to me. So I wanted to try it and introduce it. My proteges were interested in growing their audience on Substack. They asked me, "What makes this so impactful?"

The short answer is it optimizes our Substack growth with recommendations. The process is entirely under our control, with no algorithms dictating what your readers see. We decide who to recommend, and in turn, these writers might enhance our Substack strategy with their own endorsements.

This kind of best practice for promoting publications on Substack isn't just theory. The early results from beta testing have been impressive, showing that recommendations can genuinely help you grow your Substack audience.

For example, all my newsletters were recommended and received hundreds of endorsements. The most loved ones by freelance writers were my **Content Strategy, Development, & Marketing Insights**[4] which I established in 2020 as part of ILLUMINATION publications.

This newsletter was endorsed by 456 freelance writers as they found it valuable for their growth. These caring readers helped me gain 3000 additional subscribers as they recommended my newsletter.

The Recommendations feature allows us to endorse other publications when a new reader subscribes to ours. This isn't just about numbers — it's about building relationships. We can increase newsletter engagement through

---

3.   https://on.substack.com/p/recommendations

4.   https://drmehmetyildiz.substack.com/

Substack endorsements by connecting with writers we admire and want to support.

If you're serious about your Substack success, you need to start using this tool today. Leveraging recommendations can make the difference between stagnation and exponential growth.

Recommending publications on Substack is simple. Here are simple steps:

To get started with recommending other publications on Substack, first log in to your account, click on your profile picture in the top-right corner, and go to the Dashboard of your specific newsletter. For example, I choose this one.

Click on the Recommendations options, and you will see the following. So click on the Manage button.

Then, you can click on the + Add Recommendations button as shown below.

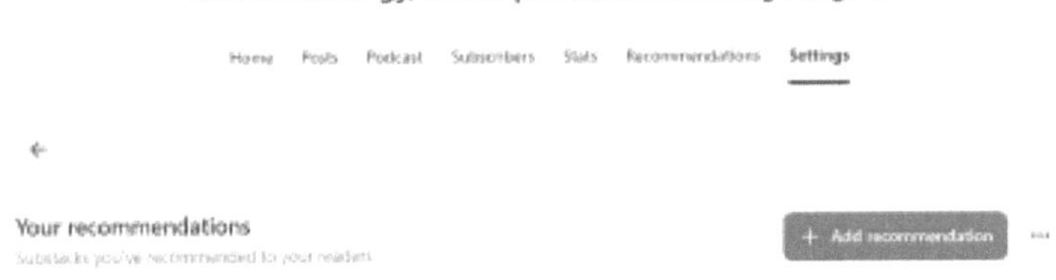

Then a window will appear, prompting the name of the publication, which you can type, and it will find it for you. Here, you can search for and select the Substacks you want to recommend. You can optionally provide a brief comment and click onthe Add recommendation.

Then it will show in my recommendations. You can edit it later by clicking on the ... (3 dots) at the left end of the entry.

After this recommendation earlier, I asked **Mike Broadly, DHSc**[5] whether he received my recommendation. He said yes and confirmed that 4 people havealready subscribed to his newsletter through this simple recommendation from my **Content Strategy, Development, & Marketing Insights**[6] newsletter.

I invite you to use this feature. It is more than just a way to promote others — it's a strategic move to enhance your Substack strategy with writer endorsements. Grow your Substack audience with recommendations and see how powerful cross-promotion can be.

Remember to go to your settings today and choose the publications you want to endorse and watch as your community grows.

Section 3: Other Sharing and Caring Options on Substack

I'd like to briefly introduce some powerful sharing features on Substack that can help you grow your audience and boost engagement.

First up, let's discuss social media sharing. This is a great way to drive more traffic to your publication and attract new subscribers. When you publish a

---

5.   https://medium.com/u/c0e38065f854

6.   https://drmehmetyildiz.substack.com/

post, you will notice share buttons for platforms like Facebook, Twitter, and LinkedIn.

Click on the last icon on the right on your published story or stories of other writers as shown below.

Substack Mastery Book: Chapter 2

What is Substack Notes, why does it matter for freelance writers, and how do you start it in 5 minutes and use it to build an audience efficiently?

AUG 25 · DR MEHMET YILDIZ

♥ 23   ⬭ 13

You will see the following options: Facebook, LinkedIn, and X. I covered Notes in detail **in the previous chapter** as it is the most important one.

All you need to do is click one of these buttons, customize your message, and share it directly with your followers. This can really help get the word out about your content.

Next is email sharing. Even in the age of social media, email remains a powerful tool for reaching your existing audience. If you really like a post, you can copy and paste the link to an email and share it with your friends or colleagues.

Then there's the use of embedded links within your posts. This is an excellent way to guide readers to related content, which can boost engagement and help with cross-promotion. To do this, simply highlight the text you want to link, click the link icon in the editor toolbar, enter the URL of the content, and apply it. It's a simple yet effective way to keep your readers exploring more of your work.

Don't forget about sharing your Substack profile page. By sharing the direct link to your profile, you make it easier for others to discover all your content. Just go to your profile page, copy the URL from your browser's address bar, and share it on social media, in emails, or even on your website.

Crossposts

One of my favourites is the Crosspost feature. If I would like to share my important posts with subscribers for mother's publications, or if I like another writer's post and introduce it to my audience, I can share the entire post with the cross-posting feature instead of embedding a post link and publishing a new post.

You can access it via ... (3 dots) at the bottom of your post.

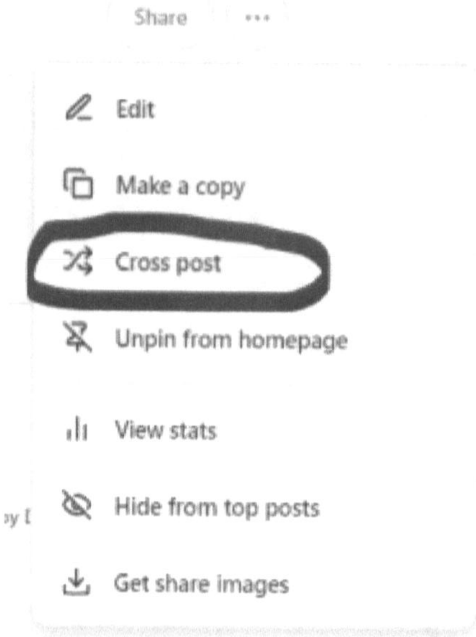

HOWEVER, IT WOULD BE useful if you could explain the reason for cross-posting it.

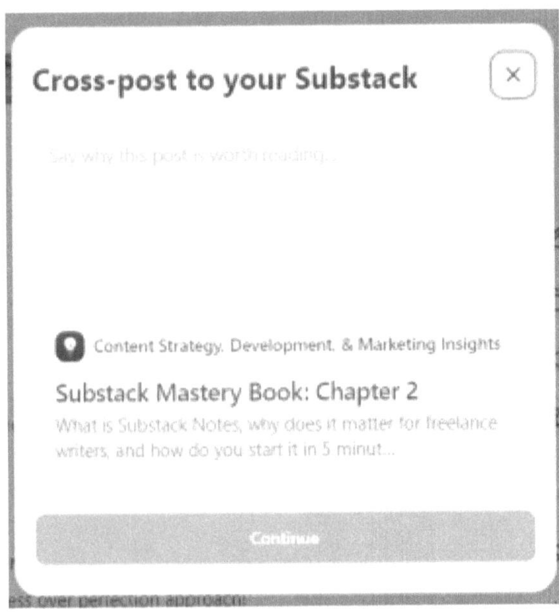

AS WRITERS, WE ARE in control. We can opt out of having our work cross-posted by other writers via the Settings page in our dashboard.

Here is a sample cross-post **Aiden (Owner of Illumination Gaming)**[7] did after reading Chapter 3 of my book in his newsletter **Technology, Gaming, Movies, and Social Media**[8]. As you can see, his not was captured in the published version on his site.

---

7.   https://medium.com/u/4a2ec49665f7

8.   https://aidenmc.substack.com/

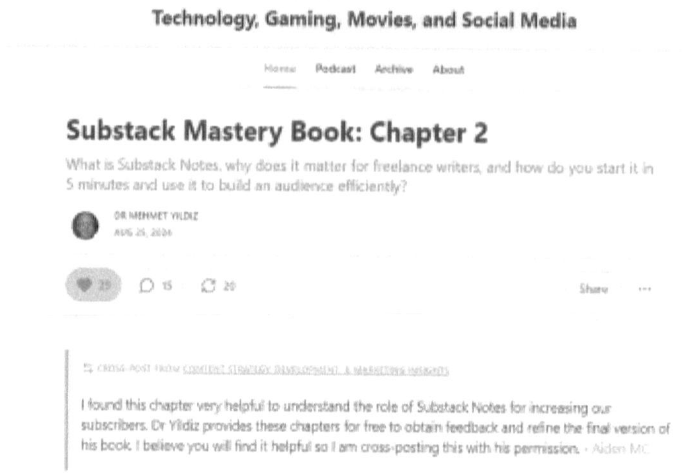

Technology, Gaming, Movies, and Social Media

Home   Podcast   Archive   About

Substack Mastery Book: Chapter 2

What is Substack Notes, why does it matter for freelance writers, and how do you start it in 5 minutes and use it to build an audience efficiently?

DR MEHMET YILDIZ
AUG 25, 2024

♥ 25   💬 15   ↻ 20   Share   •••

CROSS-POST FROM CONTENT STRATEGY DEVELOPMENT, & MARKETING INSIGHTS

I found this chapter very helpful to understand the role of Substack Notes for increasing our subscribers. Dr Yildiz provides these chapters for free to obtain feedback and refine the final version of his book. I believe you will find it helpful so I am cross-posting this with his permission. - Aiden MC

Source[9]

Referrals

Now, let's talk about the referral program. This is a fantastic way to incentivize your current subscribers to bring others on board, leading to organic growth. You can enable referrals from your Substack settings and provide a unique referral link to your subscribers. To keep the momentum going, consider rewarding your top referrers, which encourages even more sharing.

Here is what it looks like, and it gives you several options.

---

9.   https://aidenmc.substack.com/cp/148230106

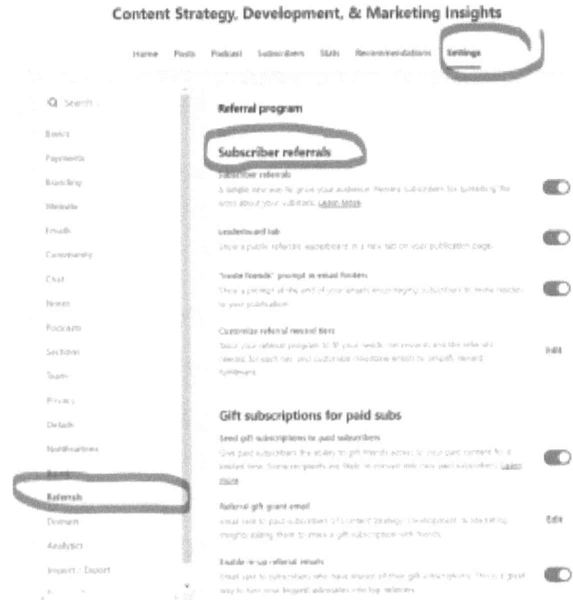

Lastly, like many other platforms, there is a sharing option to offer RSS feeds on Substack. I will cover the technical details of RSS in the advanced sections of this book.

For now briefly, RSS feeds allow readers to subscribe to your content using their preferred feed reader, making your posts more accessible. Substack automatically generates an RSS feed for your publication.

To find it, just add "/feed" to the end of your publication's URL. Promote this RSS feed on your website or social media, and explain to your readers how they can benefit from using it, especially if they prefer a clutter-free way to follow your updates.

Substack made sharing and caring very easy and effective with state-of-the-art tools. So, as creators and users, by effectively utilizing these sharing features, you can significantly enhance your Substack's growth, engagement, paid subscribers, and overall success.

Chapter 4: Crafting an impactful strategy and adaptable delivery plan to maximize subscriber growth for sustainable business value

Practical Tips for Growing Your Substack Audience: Proven Best Practices from My Experience and Observations

Summary of My High-Level Strategy and Plan: How to Develop a Winning Content Strategy for Your Substack Newsletters

1 — I Found My Niche Topics, Defined Them, and Created a Strategy and Delivery Plan

Running any business without a clear strategy and plan can be challenging, especially in a crowded and competitive space. In the vast ocean of content creation, I quickly realized that honing in on specific niche topics was vital for standing out.

This focus allowed me to attract a dedicated audience who appreciated my unique perspectives and the experiences I brought to the table within those carefully defined areas.

My approach began with identifying topics that not only excited me but also matched my expertise. For me, it was essential to choose three niches that felt natural and genuinely sparked my passion — topics I could explore in depth and consistently provide valuable insights on.

This strategy wasn't just about picking subjects; it was about crafting a plan that aligned with my goals and could sustain long-term engagement with my audience.

2 — I Tell My Personal Story in My Own Voice and Style

While I admire the stories and styles of many writers, I have learned the importance of telling my personal stories in my own voice and style. I try to find a better version of myself with pragmatic progress, refraining from perfection.

This approach is essential because sharing my journey allows me to connect more deeply with my audience. It humanizes my content, making it more relatable, memorable, and impactful for nurturing trust and loyalty.

I have chosen the idea of not shying away from sharing my struggles, successes, and everything in between. By weaving personal anecdotes with actionable advice supported by empirical evidence, I aim to create newsletters that are not only insightful and useful but also memorable and relatable.

My hope is that by using my own experiences to illustrate broader lessons, my stories will resonate with my readers in a meaningful way and perhaps inspire them to make meaningful changes in their lives.

3 — I Chose Consistency and Pragmatic Progress to Keep the Momentum

Consistency, combined with a practical approach that refrains from perfection, has become a cornerstone of my content strategy for a long time because it keeps my audience engaged and looking forward to my next piece.

Consistency builds anticipation and trust, which is crucial for maintaining a loyal following. I chose a publishing schedule that aligns with my lifestyle and commitments, ensuring I can deliver content without overwhelming myself or my readers.

To keep things fresh, I vary the topics and the frequency — sometimes weekly, bi-weekly, or even monthly — depending on what feels right.

I use tools like calendar reminders and batch writing sessions to help me stick to this schedule, allowing for flexibility when needed. This consistent approach has proven valuable, helping me grow my audience and keep them engaged over time.

4 — I Experiment with Different Content and Styles to Offer Novelty

I have discovered that experimenting with different content and styles and adding novelty helps me find a better version of myself, keeps my audience engaged, and broadens my reach.

Experimentation with novelty adds a layer of freshness and excitement to the process, which is vital for sustaining long-term creativity.

Beyond my original content, I enjoy mixing things up by incorporating interviews, guest posts, Questions and Answers (Q&As), and even adding multimedia elements like podcasts or videos to create synergy and serendipity.

Seeing how other creators keep their content dynamic inspired me to explore various formats, and this approach has been rewarding. The variety sparks my creativity and enhances audience engagement, making the whole experience more creative, productive, enriching, and fulfilling.

5 — I Stay Authentic, Honest, and True to My Voice

I learned that originality and authenticity are key success factors for creators or other professionals. Therefore, striving for originality and staying authentic has been one of the most important aspects of my journey.

Authenticity resonates deeply with readers and is crucial for building long-term trust. I have realized that being true to my voice sets me apart in a crowded space. I write how I speak and don't try to mimic others. My audience values my unique perspective even if they are presented without polishing. They appreciate the genuine voice behind my words.

I make it a point to let that authenticity and honesty shine through in everything I create. By staying true to myself no matter what ramifications my honest words might bring, I have been able to build a loyal following that connects with my content on a deeper level, which is something I prioritize with every piece I produce.

6 — I Offer Value Before Monetizing and Monetize Thoughtfully

This part of my strategy is a bit more nuanced because it is a topic often misunderstood on Substack. My approach has always been to give first, then receive. As a creator, earning income is essential to survive and thrive, but I have learned that focusing too much on revenue can be counterproductive.

Building trust and credibility with my audience was my top priority long before I even considered monetization. I wanted to ensure that what I offered my readers had real value before asking for anything in return.

I started by sharing valuable insights, tips, and stories for free, at least for the last five years. This not only helped me grow my subscriber base organically but also allowed me to establish a strong foundation of trust.

When I eventually introduced paid subscriptions a few months ago, it felt like a natural progression rather than something forced. I wanted any paid content to genuinely reflect the value I had already provided, making it feel like a fair exchange rather than a hard sell.

For those who chose to support me, especially my founding members, I offer exclusive content, deep dives, additional resources, personal consultations, and even support for their own endeavours, like promoting their goods and services if they align with my values and principles.

I have observed how some prominent creators balance free and paid content, and I have tried to emulate that balance in a way that stays true to my values. I always ensure that my paid offerings are genuinely worth the investment.

However, I feel like I made a mistake by not turning on the monetization, which delayed my growth unknowingly. Therefore, I believe it is important to turn on monetization on Substack right from the start to benefit from the algorithm.

This doesn't mean everything needs to be behind a paywall — it's entirely possible to offer all your content for free, even with monetization enabled. The key is to approach monetization thoughtfully, ensuring it aligns with the value you're already providing and feels right for both you and your audience.

7 — I Collaborate with Other Creators to Create Synergy and Serendipity

Collaborating with other creators has been a game-changer for me. It is not just about expanding my reach; it is also about finding inspiration and support along the way. I make it a point to connect with other writers and creators, whether they are in my niche, in related fields, or totally different areas.

Depending on my collaborators' needs, I engage in various ways. Sometimes, I contribute as a reader, offering feedback and support. At other times, I take on roles like editor or reviewer, helping to polish their work. I also promote their content within my own circles, which has proven to be a powerful way to support each other and grow our audiences.

Guest posts are another avenue I enjoy exploring. I either invite others to contribute to my platform or accept invitations to write for theirs. These opportunities allow me to reach new audiences and provide fresh perspectives.

One of the most effective strategies has been leveraging word of mouth. I have found that a referral program taps into my existing network and helps expand my reach organically. Collaborations and cross-promotions not only benefit me but also build a sense of community and shared success.

8 — I Use Quantitative and Qualitative Data to Refine My Strategy and Delivery Plan

Coming from both academic and business environments, I have known that tracking my progress was crucial. I have found that using both quantitative and qualitative data is key to making informed decisions. Without monitoring how things are going, it is hard to know if we are hitting the mark.

I analyze data to understand what resonates with my audience. This means looking at numbers like open rates, click-through rates, and subscriber growth, as well as paying attention to feedback and comments from readers. By regularly reviewing these analytics, I can see which posts are doing well and why.

This data-driven approach helps me fine-tune my content and strategy. If certain topics or formats perform better, I take notes and adjust my plan accordingly. It is all about finding out what matters most to my audience and making sure my content is always relevant and engaging.

By tracking the numbers and listening to constructive feedback, I continuously refine my approach to keeping my content fresh and aligned with my readers' needs, expectations, and aspirations.

Conclusions and Key Takeaways

Sharing these practices from my experience aims to illuminate how I have crafted a thriving and sustainable writing platform on Substack and beyond.

My journey has been full of learning and evolution, marked by challenges and achievements. While I acknowledge there has always been room for growth, I am appreciative of the progress made and eager to offer insights that might benefit others on similar paths.

By considering these eight principles in your strategy and delivery plan, you can tailor your approach to build a Substack newsletter that truly connects with your audience and enables a vibrant community. Here's a brief summary:

- Focus on topics you are passionate about and knowledgeable about to attract a dedicated audience and stand out in a crowded space.
- Stick to a reliable publishing schedule to build anticipation and trust, keeping your audience engaged over time.

- Build a strong connection by actively responding to feedback and creating interactive spaces for meaningful conversations.
- Prioritize delivering valuable content to build trust and establish a foundation before introducing paid options.
- Ensure that any monetization efforts reflect the value you have already provided, making paid content a natural and appealing progression.
- Keep your content dynamic and engaging by exploring different formats and incorporating multimedia elements.
- Expand your reach and gain inspiration through partnerships and cross-promotions with fellow creators.
- Regularly review quantitative and qualitative data to adjust and improve your content strategy based on audience preferences.

By thoughtfully applying these principles, you can create a newsletter that resonates with your readers and supports meaningful growth and community building. Here is **How to Write Content to Generate Steady Income**[1].

---

1.   https://medium.com/illumination/how-to-write-content-to-generate-steady-income-956c7b574b2d

Chapter 5: Editorial Excellence and Practical Tips for Self-Editing Newsletters for Cost Effectiveness and Reader Satisfaction

I have been editing content for over forty years in various roles. Editing is a crucial skill for anyone in content development and marketing, and it is essential for any profession or company that needs to communicate effectively with clients.

As a book author and academic writer, I have had the privilege of working with professional editors. When I started self-publishing, I continued to use professional editors, but the cost was steep — I had to sell at least 500 copies just to cover editorial expenses. Not everyone can afford this, but it often feels necessary.

Editing is equally important for Substack newsletters. While I can't afford a professional editor for my newsletters, some of my mentors, who earn around $10K, do hire editors who also curate their content. I have also been hired as an editor and curator for clients' newsletters, turning it into a lucrative side hustle.

Many of us experience irony when editing or proofreading. For example, when I review my own work, I often miss obvious errors, but when I edit others' content, my brain picks up even the smallest mistakes and tone or style issues.

To address this, I created a checklist that I deliberately use for each important piece. Even though I know it by heart, I still run through it quickly before hitting publish. I will share a summary of this checklist at the end of this chapter. You can customize it to suit your needs, as it is designed to be broadly applicable.

Let me give you a brief background of my self-editing approach to Substack.

When I first started self-editing my own work on Substack, I quickly realized that writing and editing are two distinct skills. Writing allows ideas to flow freely, but editing is where the real work begins.

Self-reading is about shaping those raw ideas into something coherent, engaging, and polished. Balancing creativity with structure, as both the writer and the editor, was a challenge — but also a rewarding experience.

Editing is different than proofreading. So, it is not just about correcting grammar or fixing typos. It is about making sure that every word serves a purpose, cutting out the fluff, and getting to the heart of what you want to say and what your readers want to read.

I highlighted the importance of **clarity, brevity, and impact in a recent story**[1] as an attribute to Tim Denning's recent story on ILLUMINATION, revealing the secrets of the top 1% of successful writers.

Self-editing meant learning to be ruthless with my own work, trimming unnecessary details, and tightening up sentences until they were as clear and concise as possible.

But editing also required me to step back and see the bigger picture. I kept asking three powerful questions:

Is the overall structure of my piece working?

Do the ideas flow logically from one point to the next?

Is the pacing right?

I had to ask myself these questions as I worked through each draft, making sure that the story I was telling was compelling and easy to follow.

One of my most important lessons was that editing is a process. It takes time, and it requires multiple rounds of revisions. I would write a draft, let it sit for a while, and then return to it with fresh eyes.

This pragmatic approach gave me the perspective I needed to spot inconsistencies, weak arguments, or areas that needed more development. It wasn't always easy, but the result was always worth the effort.

Through trial and error, I developed techniques that helped me refine my content and bring it to its full potential. These techniques became the foundation of my editorial process, guiding me through each piece I wrote.

---

1.   https://medium.com/p/a360db451e0a

Practical Self-Editing Techniques

One technique that proved invaluable was reading my work out loud. This simple step helped me catch awkward phrasing, repetitive words, and sentences that didn't flow as smoothly as I thought they did.

Hearing the words spoken aloud made it easier to identify areas that needed improvement, allowing me to fine-tune the rhythm and cadence of my writing.

Another technique was to focus on the reader's experience. As I edited, I constantly asked myself:

How will this come across to someone who isn't familiar with the topic?

Is the information clear and accessible?

Am I engaging the reader from start to finish?

By putting myself in the reader's shoes, I was able to make my content more relatable and impactful.

For years, I have used a unique and challenging technique called **backward sentence reading** to overcome **cognitive distortions**[2] — a technique I developed while studying cognitive science, particularly the concept of cognitive dissonance, a common error in our complex minds.

Another important approach for me was the value of taking breaks during the editing process. After spending hours on a piece, it is easy to become blind to its flaws. Stepping away for a while—a few hours or days—gave me the distance I needed to see my work with fresh eyes. When I returned, I could approach the editing process with renewed focus and clarity.

However, perhaps the most important technique I developed was learning to let go. As writers, we can become attached to certain phrases, sentences, or even entire paragraphs that we love but don't serve the piece as a whole.

Editing requires a willingness to cut what isn't working, even if it means letting go of something we are proud of. It's about serving the story, not our egos.

I strive for excellence, not perfection.

In my younger years, I was a perfectionist, which ruined my physical and mental health. **As I documented in a personal story**[3], moving from perfection to excellence with meaningful progress by accepting my imperfections, a heavy

---

2.   https://medium.com/sensible-biohacking-transhumanism/notice-and-fix-your-cognitive-distortions-to-live-healthier-and-happier-9b3c1b51806c

load disappeared from my shoulders. I use the concept of MVP (**minimal viable product**[4]) concept to make necessary progress in my personal and professional life.

Editing is an ongoing journey. No piece of writing is perfect. As human beings, we are imperfect. However, with each edit, it gets closer to excellence. My goal as a self-editor was to ensure that every piece I published was the best possible — a reflection of my commitment to quality and my respect for my readers.

I strive to find a better version of myself in each new piece. This process wasn't just about improving the writing but building trust with my audience. When readers see that we have taken the time to craft a well-edited piece, they are more likely to engage with our content and return for more. It shows that we value their time and are committed to delivering something worthwhile.

Editorial excellence also meant being open to feedback. While I edited my own work, I also sought input from others—whether a trusted friend, my wife, my grown-up kids, a fellow writer, or even my loyal readers. This external perspective helped me see things I might have missed and offered new insights that strengthened my work.

Over time, as I honed my self-editing skills, I noticed an improvement in my writing. My ideas became clearer, my arguments stronger, and my voice more refined. Self-editing was beyond a task I had to complete. It became integral to my creative process, shaping how I approached each new piece.

To recap, as both a writer and a self-editor, I discovered that the two roles are deeply interconnected. Writing is the creative spark, but editing is the craftsmanship that turns that spark into something tangible, something that can be shared with the world. It's a balance of creativity and discipline, of passion and precision.

In the end, editorial excellence isn't about perfection. It's about striving to make our work the best it can be while always keeping the reader in mind. It's about welcoming the process, learning from each experience, and continuously evolving as a writer and a self-editor.

3.   https://medium.com/sensible-biohacking-transhumanism/why-i-find-perfection-in-imperfection-533c706aa47f

4.   https://medium.com/sensible-biohacking-transhumanism/perfections-road-led-nowhere-mvp-became-my-springboard-to-flourish-b36c4d4b0535

This chapter of my Substack journey taught me that self-editing is not just a skill — it is an art. And like any art, it requires dedication, practice, and a willingness to always seek improvement. The better I become at self-editing, the more confident I feel in my writing, and the more meaningful my connection with my readers becomes.

A Sample Generic Self-Editing Checklist

Creating a self-editing checklist is a great way to improve the quality of your Substack newsletters. Here's a list of 20 essential items to focus on for your self-editing process that you can customize:

- Ensure each newsletter has a clear central theme or message.
- Start with a hook that grabs the reader's attention.
- Check that ideas flow logically from one paragraph to the next.
- Eliminate unnecessary words, phrases, or sentences.
- Keep paragraphs short and focused, typically 3–5 sentences.
- Use plain language that's easy to understand; avoid jargon.
- Write in an active voice to make your writing more direct and engaging.
- Ensure your tone and style are consistent throughout, reflecting your brand or personal style.
- Write as if you are having a conversation with the reader.
- Include personal anecdotes or insights to connect with readers.
- Mix short and long sentences to create rhythm and maintain reader interest.
- Use subheadings to break up content and guide the reader through your newsletter and make them captivating, intriguing, and memorable.
- Use bullet points or numbered lists for clarity and emphasis.
- Review for common grammar mistakes (e.g., subject-verb agreement, proper tense usage).
- Run a spell check and manually review for homophones (e.g., their/there/they're).
- Check punctuation, especially commas, periods, and quotation marks.
- Ensure consistent use of fonts, sizes, and colours.

- Check that all hyperlinks work and lead to the correct pages.
- Ensure images are properly aligned and sized within the newsletter. More importantly, ensure **all images are copyright-free to protect yourself.**[5]
- Conclude with a clear call to action (subscribe, share, comment, join chat).

After reviewing this checklist, give your newsletter a final read-through to see how it flows and whether it keeps your interest from start to finish.

If you are writing stories or articles, I also provided **a practical checklist for beginners**[6]. If you are an advanced writer or a book author, you may also check out **this comprehensive checklist,**[7] which I created for writers who want to increase their chances of boosting on the platform.

By thoughtfully applying these self-editing principles, you can create a newsletter that resonates with your readers and supports meaningful growth and community building. Here is **How to Write Content to Generate Steady Income**[8].

---

5. https://medium.com/p/62e402f4139a

6. https://medium.com/illumination/level-1-a-practical-checklist-for-content-quality-improvement-96e7c2313f69

7. https://medium.com/illumination/enhance-the-chance-of-boosting-by-enriching-the-quality-of-your-content-with-practical-steps-cdf64b92ff15

8. https://medium.com/illumination/how-to-write-content-to-generate-steady-income-956c7b574b2d

Chapter 6: How to Configure and Maintain Privacy of Substack Publications with Compelling Reasons

I have written extensively about privacy across various contexts because it is a crucial element of my work in science and technology. The importance of privacy has only grown with the rise of the internet, the emergence of cybersecurity concerns, and the global increase in cybercrime. Privacy issues caused major scams that happened to me in 2022, causing me to lose some portion of my retirement funds and **leading me to seek a lifeline.**[1]

Some regions, particularly Europe, have taken significant steps to address privacy issues, enacting strict regulations that challenge tech giants like Facebook, Google, Microsoft, and X. In Australia, **where I live**[2], both government and private organizations pay utmost importance to privacy.

Recently, **Facebook accidentally suspended my 20-year-old account**[3]. It concerned me and hurt my feelings. I decided to do the appeal process but found it intrusive. So, I included a poll in the story about whether I should appeal or not. The exact question was, "Should I apply for an appeal to Facebook using my personally identifiable data or not?" I gave four options. 60% of my friends did not want me to appeal. Only 20% said yes.

---

1. https://medium.com/sensible-biohacking-transhumanism/heres-why-i-called-a-lifeline-first-time-in-my-life-today-9b480b9e22c3

2. https://medium.com/sensible-biohacking-transhumanism/why-i-choose-to-live-in-australia-f899da52d3ea

3. https://medium.com/illumination/why-facebook-suspended-my-20-year-old-account-abruptly-today-0636d9028789

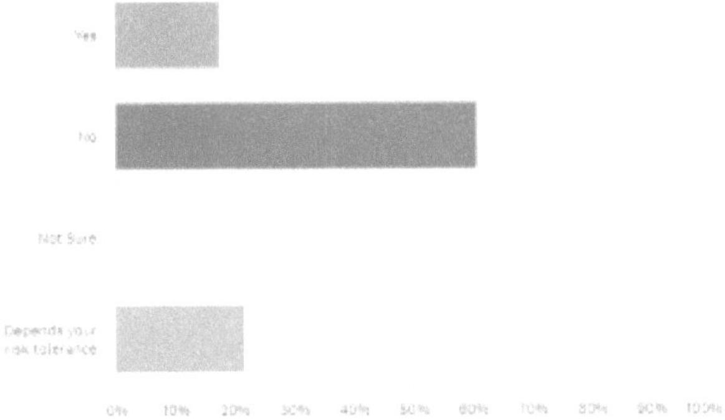

Fortunately, with the help of my network, the issue was escalated to higher levels at Facebook, **where it was resolved amicably**[4], accompanied by an apology.

Back to Substack

Given that this book focuses on a specific platform, I will concentrate on privacy management for writers. Substack, a platform I have been following closely, has a comprehensive privacy policy regularly updated to address emerging concerns. For instance, their **most recent update was on August 28, 2024.**[5]

The platform takes privacy seriously, empowering creators with robust tools to protect their personal information. At the same time, it offers flexibility for writers who prioritize global visibility over privacy and are willing to take calculated risks.

Personally, I find myself somewhere in the middle. Certain aspects of privacy are vital to me, while others are less critical. Everyone has different needs, so Substack allows for customization to suit individual preferences.

Writers must understand and tailor these settings on Substack to maintain control over their content, protect their privacy, and ensure their work effectively reaches the right audience.

How to Configure Privacy for a Substack Publication

---

4. https://medium.com/illumination-curated/finally-mark-zuckerberg-answered-my-plea-thanks-to-my-global-contacts-c5f191d0e704

5. https://substack.com/privacy

You can access and customize these privacy settings directly from your publication's settings page, as shown in the following screenshot. So click on Dashboard and then Setting.

Then, you click on the Settings tab as shown below.

Basics

Payments

Branding

Website

Emails

Community

Chat

Notes

Podcasts

Sections

Team

Privacy

Details

Notifications

Boost

Referrals

Domain

Analytics

Import / Export

Danger Zone

CHOOSING THE PRIVACY tab will open the following window.

Privacy

Private mode
In private mode, only people you approve can subscribe and view your posts. Existing subscribers will not be affected.

Allow cross-posting
Allow free posts to be cross-posted to other publications. Cross-posting can help expose your publication get discovered by new audiences.

Allow listing on Substack.com
Allow visitors to the Substack website to search for and discover your publication

Allow search engines to index paywalled content
Allows excerpts from paywalled posts to show up in search results. Non-subscribers will still see a paywall when they click through to your website.

Allow AI training
Allows platforms like ChatGPT and Google Bard to train on your content. Disabling may limit your discoverability on these platforms.

Show approximate subscriber count
Displays your rough subscriber count in places like your profile and welcome page. This can help boost free subscriber conversion.

Custom terms of service
Add your own terms of service to your publication.
Customize

Custom privacy policy
Add your own privacy policy to your publication.
Customize

An Overview of Privacy Options on Substack

I will briefly explain each setting and why it matters, drawing from my experience and observations. These settings aren't simply black and white. Therefore, Substack offers us the flexibility to toggle them on or off based on our unique preferences and needs.

Private Mode

Private mode allows us to limit access to your content to only those subscribers you approve. This is particularly important for writers who share sensitive, personal, or niche content not intended for a general audience.

By using private mode, we can control who accesses our content, reducing the risk of it being shared publicly or falling into the wrong hands. This can be crucial for maintaining a safe and secure writing environment.

For example, a writer covering sensitive political topics might enable private mode to ensure that only trusted subscribers can view their posts, thus protecting themselves and their readers from potential backlash or harassment.

Allow Cross-Posting

As I introduced **in Chapter 3,**[6] cross-posting can increase our exposure by allowing our free posts to be shared on other publications. However, if you want to maintain tight control over where and how your content is distributed, you may want to disable this feature.

For example, if you prefer to keep your content within a specific community or platform, disabling cross-posting can help you manage where your work appears and prevent it from being distributed without your consent.

By controlling cross-posting, you can prevent your work from being shared in contexts you didn't intend, helping to maintain the integrity and original purpose of your content. I personally allow cross-posting as I have no concerns about my content going to extended communities.

Allow Listing on Substack.com

Being listed on Substack.com makes our publications discoverable by a broader audience, which can be beneficial for growing our readership. However, it also means that our work is more publicly visible, which might not be desirable for all writers.

For example, a writer who values a smaller, more engaged audience might prefer to remain unlisted to avoid attracting a general audience that may not align with their content's purpose.

If privacy is a priority, you might remain unlisted, limiting your exposure to only those who already know about your publication or who find it through direct links.

Allow Search Engines to Index Paywalled Content

This setting lets search engines index snippets of our paywalled content, which can help attract new subscribers by showing them a preview of what's behind the paywall. However, it also means that excerpts of our content are available on the internet.

---

6.   https://medium.com/illumination/substack-mastery-book-chapter-3-e13b575f1598

For example, a writer who relies on paywalled content for income might enable this feature to attract potential subscribers by giving them a taste of what they're missing. On the other hand, a writer who values complete content control might disable it to keep their work fully protected behind the paywall.

Disabling this feature ensures that your paywalled content remains completely inaccessible unless someone subscribes, maintaining exclusivity and protecting your intellectual property.

Allow AI Training

I have written a detailed story about it before, as many writers in my publications have asked me to do so. You can read the details in a story titled **Should I "Block AI Training" on Substack? : A Concise/Practical Guide**[7].

In short, when we allow AI platforms like ChatGPT and Google Gemini to train on our content, we contribute to the data these models use to generate responses. This can increase our content's visibility, but it also means our work is being used to train algorithms without direct compensation.

For example, a writer who values broad exposure might opt to allow AI training, understanding that it could lead to their work being referenced more widely. However, another writer concerned about how their work is used might disable this feature to avoid contributing to AI training.

So, by disabling AI training, you ensure that your content isn't being used by AI models without your explicit consent, thus keeping your intellectual property under tighter control.

Show Approximate Subscriber Count

Displaying your subscriber count can add social proof and help boost conversions, as potential subscribers see that others are interested in your work. However, some writers might prefer to keep this information private.

For example, a writer with a large subscriber base might display this number to encourage others to join, while a writer with a smaller or niche audience might choose to hide it to avoid discouraging potential subscribers.

So, by choosing not to display your subscriber count, you maintain control over how your publication is perceived, especially in the early stages when numbers might be lower. I personally allow the number of subscribers on my publications.

---

7.   https://medium.com/illumination/should-i-block-ai-training-on-substack-a-concise-practical-guide-01daa36dc822

Custom Terms of Service and Privacy Policy

Custom service terms and privacy policies allow you to set clear guidelines for how your content can be used and what rights your subscribers have. This is important for protecting your work and ensuring that your audience understands the rules of engagement.

For example, a writer offering exclusive content might use custom terms to specify how their work can be shared or referenced, thus protecting their intellectual property and clarifying the terms for subscribers.

Customizing these policies ensures that we aren't solely dependent on Substack's default terms, which may not fully address our specific needs or the nature of our content. Although I haven't yet created my own policy, I plan to do so, particularly for my technology excellence publication, where I utilize personal research data from my labs.

When I develop this policy, I will include it as an addendum in the next version of this book to keep my readers informed. Crafting a policy requires time and careful consideration, as it involves evaluating various factors from multiple perspectives and thoroughly weighing the pros and cons.

Conclusions and Takeaways

When discussing this topic with privacy experts, they said that customizing our privacy settings on Substack isn't just a matter of personal preference—it is a crucial step in protecting our intellectual property, managing our online presence, and ensuring that our content is shared with the intended audience.

As writers, our work might touch on sensitive topics, personal experiences, or proprietary research. Protecting this work is essential to maintaining its integrity and ensuring it reaches the right people in the right way.

Each setting on Substack provides a delicate balance between gaining exposure and maintaining privacy. Whether you seek to expand your audience globally or protect your content from unauthorized use, these settings give you the control needed to navigate the digital landscape effectively.

Choosing to enable or disable these options should be a strategic decision aligned with your goals and the specific nature of your work. So, you may consider them as part of your strategy, **which I covered in Chapter 4.**[8]

By thoroughly understanding and carefully adjusting these settings, you can create a safer, more controlled environment for your writing.

---

8. https://medium.com/illumination/substack-mastery-book-chapter-4-f5829191e7ae

This enhances your peace of mind and allows you to focus on your creative process, knowing that your privacy is being actively managed.

Ultimately, this proactive approach leads to greater satisfaction and long-term success in your writing journey, ensuring that your work remains protected and respected in an increasingly connected world.

By thoughtfully applying these privacy principles, you can create a newsletter that resonates with your readers and supports meaningful growth and community building. Here is **How to Write Content to Generate Steady Income**[9].

---

9. https://medium.com/illumination/how-to-write-content-to-generate-steady-income-956c7b574b2d

Chapter 7: LinkedIn Is Goldmine for Substack Creators for Growing Audience

I have been using social media tools since their inception, leveraging my background as a designer of social systems in technology and enterprise architecture roles years ago. Social media is **a double-edged sword** [1] — when used correctly, it can bring tremendous benefits, but when misused, it can lead to serious health issues.

In my writing journey, I have used social media to create visibility for my content, including articles and books. One of the most intriguing aspects has been experimenting with various social media platforms to market my Substack newsletters and posts. I started with LinkedIn, Quora, X Premium, Facebook, and Reddit.

However, it didn't take long to realize that while these platforms are great for visibility, LinkedIn stands out as the most effective for converting free

---

1. https://medium.com/illumination-blog/social-media-is-a-double-edged-sword-for-creators-but-we-can-use-it-for-good-outcomes-1551e734a35c

subscribers into paid ones. This insight comes not only from my own experience but also from anecdotes shared by my collaborators.

While I plan to cover social media tools comprehensively in a future chapter, today, I want to focus on LinkedIn's key strengths, supported by practical examples.

What I'm offering to beta readers is not exactly how the book is structured but rather an adaptive approach. To ensure it is useful to a broad audience, I have rearranged the sequence of chapters and tailored the content to highlight the most effective tools based on readers' needs.

Why I Consider LinkedIn as a Powerful Conversion Tool

ON LINKEDIN, PROFESSIONALS connect, learn, and invest in personal growth. The platform's focus on business thought leadership and professional development means the audience is already primed for high-quality content. They seek value, expertise, and insights to help them in their careers or businesses.

I have relatively more followers on LinkedIn than on other social media platforms. A few months ago, when I introduced my newsletters and shared my Substack posts on LinkedIn, I noticed something remarkable—80% of my paid subscribers came from LinkedIn. You may wonder why.

LinkedIn users see the value in investing in content that delivers actionable insights and in-depth analysis from trusted content developers. They are cautious about their time, understand the worth of quality information, and are willing to pay for getting the optimal value.

LinkedIn's algorithm is designed to boost content that engages and educates. My posts reached a relevant audience, leading to meaningful interactions, discussions, and, ultimately, conversions.

The credibility I have built over years of sharing knowledge on LinkedIn on my expertise areas directly translated into trust, making it easier to convert readers into paying subscribers for my three newsletters covering technology, content strategy, and health/wellbeing matters.

While other social media platforms play their role in building awareness, LinkedIn's professional environment and the intent-driven nature of its users make it unparalleled for driving paid subscriptions.

If you are serious about growing your Substack and converting subscribers to paid ones, you might focus your efforts on LinkedIn. It is a platform where content meets commitment, and that's a winning combination for anyone looking to turn readers into paying members.

What I Did Differently on LinkedIn

LINKEDIN OFFERS MANY remarkable features that make it easy for professionals to showcase their work and create visibility for their content.

One of the most impactful features for me has been the ability to add my Substack newsletter to my experience section. This simple yet powerful addition allows me to present my newsletters to my followers, subscribers, and anyone visiting my profile.

As shown in the screen capture below, I have added Substack as my self-employment company and linked it to my three newsletters, each with its respective start date and a brief explanation. This approach has been instrumental in reaching a wider audience and converting free subscribers into paid ones.

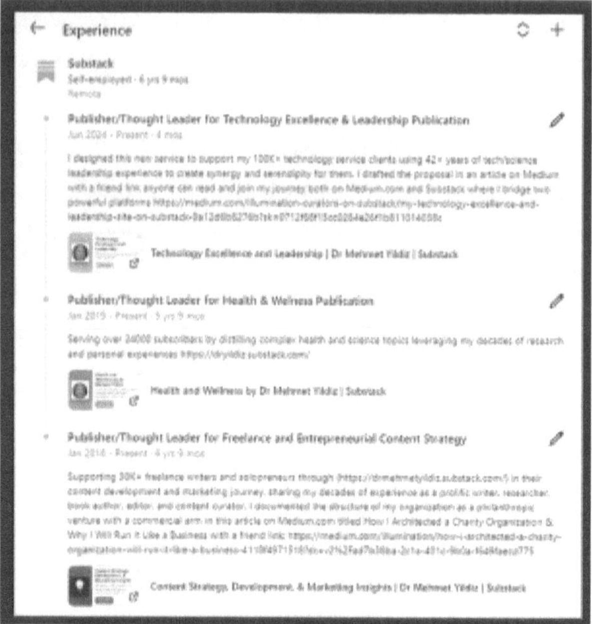

Screenshot from my LinkedIn profile[2]

The Power of LinkedIn Newsletters

AS A GREAT CONTENT dissemination platform, LinkedIn offers a free newsletter service where creators share their articles directly with their subscribers. Recently, I created a free newsletter and started sharing my articles and curated collections regularly.

In a short time, the newsletter gained over 3000 subscribers who got my posts in their inboxes. New visitors can also see them in article format on the site and can subscribe to it. When subscribers share the posts, it makes a ripple effect as the more sharing and engagement a post gets the more it is amplified by the platform.

Here is how my newsletter looks on my LinkedIn profile.

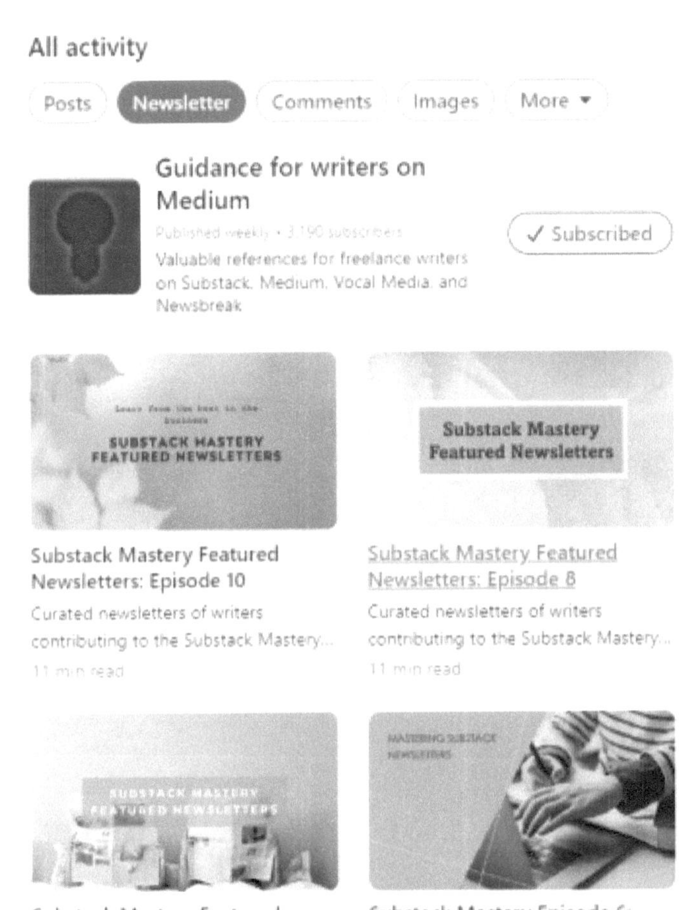

Link to my LinkedIn Newsletter Guidance for Writers on Medium[3]

The only problem with LinkedIn newsletters is we cannot change names, or it is not recommended by Linked as they think that it would confuse the subscribers and they might unsubscribe. So, I followed their advice and kept the original name as I couldn't create a new newsletter with a name. My intention was to call it Substack Mastery, which is the name of my book.

---

3.   https://www.linkedin.com/in/mehmetyildiz/recent-activity/newsletter/

The Power of LinkedIn Collaboration Groups

ANOTHER FANTASTIC OPTION I discovered on LinkedIn as a supplementary resource for my newsletter is LinkedIn Groups. This powerful feature adds a more interactive and collaborative dimension to the platform.

Two weeks ago, I created a group and invited about 2,000 connections out of my 25,262 followers. Remarkably, over 1,700 have already joined, eager to share their work and engage with the Substack newsletters of other writers.

Although I only launched the group a few weeks ago, it's been growing rapidly as more Substack writers are drawn to this community activity.

Link to the Substack Mastry LinkedIn Group[4]

LINKEDIN PROVIDED ME with a snapshot of job titles who joined my group. As you can see, some of them are writers, editors, publishers, company founders, and CEOs. They are all professionals compared to X or Facebook.

How to Post to LinkedIn Groups

FIRST, YOU NEED TO join the group. Some groups are private, so some diligence and approval are required. However, I made my group public so anyone can join and network. Unlike Twitter or Facebook, I have never had

---

4. https://www.linkedin.com/groups/14501005/

any issues on LinkedIn, so my trust is high on this platform to open my group to the public.

Once you join the group, all you need is to copy and paste the link of your story or Substack newsletter with a brief note in a message box on the top of the group, as shown below.

AS YOU CAN SEE FROM the message box, you can do three things. You can link your article or newsletter, which LinkedIn can embed as a great-looking post. You can add media like photos, videos, or podcasts. You can also create a poll, as I will show below.

Here is a sample post I shared in the Substack Mastery featuring an interview I conducted with **Veronica Llorca-Smith**[5].

---

5.   **https://medium.com/u/77698eaeabab**

Link to the post at Substack Mastery LinkedIn Group[6]

If you missed the interview on this platform, here is the link. This is a community-building activity as Veronica shared her strategy and approach to converting her free subscribers to paid ones. She earned $10,000 last month, as I linked the artifact in the interview story.

---

6.   **https://www.linkedin.com/feed/update/**
    urn:li:activity:7236689280872386560?utm_source=share&utm_medium=member_desktop

<u>Interview with Veronica Llorca-Smith[7]</u>

<u>Professional Speaker, Award-Winning Author, Bestselling Substack Creator, Ironman Triathlete, Polyglot (6 Languages)...[8]</u>

How to Create Media-Enriched Posts to Get More Impressions

HERE IS A MEDIA EXAMPLE for a LinkedIn post. I added the cover of my book with relevant links to it. You can add photos and videos via the media option. From my experience, any post with media is better distributed by the LinkedIn algorithm. They perform much better than simple link embeds. So please take advantage of this excellent feature to reach a broader audience by getting more impressions that can lead to conversions.

Creating Polls to Learn from Collaborators

IN THE PREVIOUS SURVEY, 12% of writers prefer Medium as their sole platform, and 42% lean toward Substack, but the good news is that 46%, like me, prefer using both platforms.

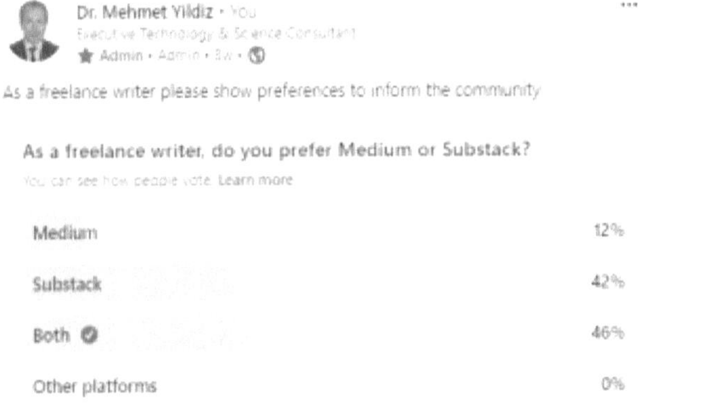

Inspiring and Uplifting Your Teammates

YOU CAN ALSO POST INSPIRATIONAL messages for your friends and colleagues, as **Michelle Mariscal[9]** kindly did for me. These types of

---

7.   https://medium.com/illumination-curated/interview-with-veronica-llorca-smith-1a0c26f2ec86

8.   https://medium.com/illumination-curated/interview-with-veronica-llorca-smith-1a0c26f2ec86

easy-to-create posts can create serendipity while uplifting your friends, colleagues, and collaborators on LinkedIn. You can also amplify them on their social media platforms like X, Facebook, Quora, Reddit, or Instagram. You can even share them on Substack Notes by linking newsletters of your favourite writers.

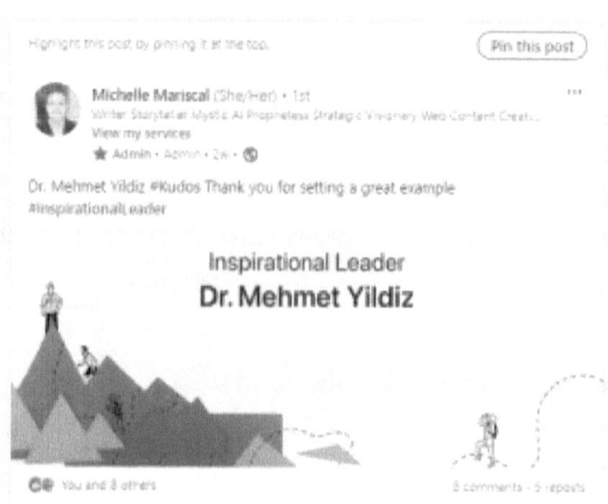

Conclusions and Key Takeaways

THERE ARE SO MANY FEATURES of LinkedIn that will go beyond the scope of this chapter. So I suggest you start exploring all those features. One of our inspiring writers, Tim Denning, articulated the value of LinkedIn for creators, and he even created a training program about it as it is a very effective platform with a proven track record.

Tim made a significant impact on Substack, like Veronica being a best-selling Substack author. Therefore, I interviewed Tim again to pick his great brain and give my readers insights into his amazing experience. Here is the link to his inspiring and empowering interview which he shared his experience generously.

[Why Did I Interview My Aussie Friend Tim Denning Again on Medium & Substack?](10)

---

9. https://medium.com/u/e56bd9bb495a

10. https://medium.com/illumination/why-did-i-interview-my-aussie-friend-tim-denning-again-on-medium-substack-f44257d456ef

This highly followed writer, known for his viral content on Medium, is now getting 50 times more views on Substack...[11]

I will write a more comprehensive story about other features of LinkedIn that I use for personal and professional growth. I see it as a serendipity machine any creator can use and benefit from. It is free and well-moderated.

LinkedIn Is a Goldmine for Substack Creators! Social media is good for promoting Substack, but nothing easier can beat LinkedIn in converting free subscribers to paid ones. The next good one is YouTube, which is a bit harder than LinkedIn.

To this end, our hardworking and brilliant team has now created a Substack YouTube channel to leverage the power of videos, audio, storytelling, and blogging. Our media coordinator **Aiden (Owner of Illumination Gaming)**[12] will be leading this initiative. He created **a short video**[13] describing the services we will provide. Join our exciting journey to reap the benefits of community spirit.

---

11. https://medium.com/illumination/why-did-i-interview-my-aussie-friend-tim-denning-again-on-medium-substack-f44257d456ef

12.   **https://medium.com/u/4a2ec49665f7**

13.   **https://www.youtube.com/watch?v=K712oUIQsPU**

Chapter 8: Why Readers Pay for Substack Newsletters and What Type of Content Fails to Attract Subscribers

This chapter will address a critical question asked by many Substack newsletter creators: "What makes readers willing to pay for content?" and "What are the critical points to increase conversion rate?" After conducting extensive research by interviewing successful writers, as well as those struggling to attract paid subscribers, I have gathered valuable insights.

My expertise in this area comes from my privilege of reviewing comprehensive research conducted by a leading content subscription service. This research included both quantitative surveys and qualitative interviews, examining why some readers upgrade to paid services and why others cancel.

This topic is very comprehensive. Thus, in this chapter, I will distil key findings into two sections. First, I will outline eight reasons why readers are willing to pay for content, providing practical insights to help you shape your strategy. The second section will explore seven reasons why readers might be reluctant to pay, which you can address with straightforward questions.

Part 1: What Type of Newsletters Have Highest Conversion Rates

1. Exclusive and High-Quality Content

HIGH-QUALITY, EXCLUSIVE content is valuable, but understanding what makes content high-quality and exclusive can be tricky because these terms can be subjective. Instead of just defining them, I want to give some concrete examples.

Some subscribers value content that delivers more than just basic information. They are willing to pay for reports, analyses, detailed examinations of complicated subjects, and insights that offer a deeper understanding and exclusive perspectives on topics that matter to them.

In my work, I have been hired to create detailed reports and analyses on specific topics within my area of expertise. For some of these reports, clients were willing to pay $10K for just one in-depth analysis. This shows that people are willing to invest in content that offers more than what's freely available.

Now, if a subscriber knows that my report is valued at $10K, they will not hesitate to subscribe to my entire content for $5 a month. So, selling this business proposition is simple.

2. Technical and Subject Matter Expertise, Authority, Deep Dives, and In-Depth Reporting

SOME READERS WANT TO consume first-hand information directly produced by subject matter experts, specialists, or researchers. So, on Substack, newsletters are an ideal platform for experts to share their unique perspectives on various topics, like technology, health, medicine, wellness, nutrition, law, leadership, journalism, or finance.

Long-form investigations are in demand. Subscribers appreciate the depth and detail that comes with long-form investigative journalism. These newsletters often delve into complex topics, providing thorough research and analysis that goes beyond surface-level coverage. Subscribers appreciate content from credible sources with deep knowledge and experience.

Like myself, I have also seen health professionals who share their expertise on wellness and medical trends through their newsletters. They offer practical advice and research-backed information that readers find valuable, especially when it comes to making informed decisions about their health.

One of my colleagues, a seasoned financial analyst, used his newsletter to provide exclusive market predictions and financial strategies. Subscribers were eager to pay for these insights because they offered a deeper understanding of market trends that couldn't be easily found elsewhere.

Another example is a tech expert I know who writes about emerging technologies and their implications for businesses. His newsletter features detailed reviews and forecasts about the latest tech developments. Subscribers value this content because it helps them stay ahead in a fast-evolving field.

3. Personalized and Niche Content

FOR THOSE WITH UNIQUE or specialized hobbies, Substack newsletters provide a way to access highly relevant and engaging information.

From my experience and observations, I know of a newsletter dedicated to rare coin collecting, a niche but passionate community. The newsletter offers detailed guides on rare finds, valuation tips, and market trends. Subscribers who are avid collectors are willing to pay for this content because it provides specialized knowledge and updates that are not readily available elsewhere.

I have seen newsletters covering niche hobbies like vintage typewriters or rare board games. These newsletters offer expert tips, historical insights, and community news. Subscribers are often dedicated hobbyists who appreciate content that is deeply focused on their interests, making it worth their investment.

Another example is a travel enthusiast who runs a Substack focused on off-the-beaten-path destinations. Their newsletter includes in-depth travel guides, local insights, and personal recommendations for unique experiences. Subscribers who crave unusual travel adventures find this highly valuable because it caters to their specific interests and provides insider knowledge.

4. Unique Perspectives with Valuable Life Lessons

ONE COMPELLING REASON readers subscribe to paid newsletters is the opportunity to gain unique perspectives with in-depth analysis that they can't find elsewhere. These newsletters provide fresh insights that challenge conventional thinking and offer valuable counterpoints to mainstream narratives.

For example, a newsletter I follow regularly provides a distinctive view of global economic trends, offering analysis that diverges from typical media coverage. This type of content appeals to subscribers looking for nuanced discussions rather than standard discussions.

Some newsletters specialize in offering thorough examinations of emerging trends. I have seen newsletters that focus on tech innovation, providing detailed analysis of new technologies and their potential impact, which is often missing in broader tech coverage. Subscribers value these insights because they help them stay ahead of the curve.

A newsletter I enjoy critically examines widely accepted theories and practices and offers alternative viewpoints. For instance, a finance-focused newsletter might question traditional investment strategies and propose innovative methods based on recent research. This critical analysis can be especially valuable to subscribers looking for more than just mainstream opinions.

Some newsletters feature personal anecdotes and experiences that offer a unique perspective on various issues. I have seen newsletters where creators share their journeys through challenges or successes, providing personal and profound insights. Subscribers appreciate these authentic stories as they offer a more relatable and engaging viewpoint.

6. Early Access and Updates to Ongoing Projects

SOME READERS SUBSCRIBE to paid newsletters to get early access to valuable content for them, keeping them ahead of trends and developments. Offering exclusive previews or updates can be a powerful draw for those eager to stay in the loop.

In one of my client projects, I have seen companies pay for early access to industry reports that will later become public. Being the first to receive these insights can give businesses a competitive edge, helping them make informed decisions before the rest of the market catches on.

Some creators share behind-the-scenes updates on their work with paying subscribers. For example, I have followed newsletters where fiction authors release sneak previews of chapters from their upcoming books. This gives readers a sense of involvement and excitement as they glimpse the creative process before anyone else.

Some newsletters offer early access to new product launches, from tech gadgets to lifestyle products. A friend runs a newsletter where she previews new designs for her handmade goods to paying subscribers before releasing them to the public. This creates buzz and makes her subscribers feel like VIPs, with the chance to purchase before the general public.

I have seen Substack writers provide subscribers with early access to tickets for live events, webinars, or workshops. This is especially valuable for readers who want to participate in limited-availability experiences, ensuring they don't miss out.

Staying ahead of trends can be crucial in niche markets like cryptocurrency, NFTs, or fashion. Newsletters that offer early updates on emerging technologies or upcoming industry changes give subscribers an advantage, helping them make strategic moves or investments before the wider public is informed.

7. Curated and Educational Content

SOME PAID NEWSLETTERS provide curated content, saving readers time by delivering the most relevant and valuable information directly to their inboxes. These roundups are perfect for subscribers who want to stay informed without sifting through countless sources.

Curated and educational content gives subscribers the best of both worlds — time-saving curation and actionable learning resources. Whether it's a roundup of top news or hands-on tutorials, this type of content keeps readers informed and constantly growing, making it well worth paying for.

A colleague of mine subscribes to a paid newsletter in the tech industry that delivers a weekly roundup of the most important news, trends, and articles. I've worked on similar newsletters that offer subscribers condensed versions of in-depth research reports or global news in sectors like finance or healthcare.

By summarizing and curating only the most significant pieces, readers get the highlights without the overwhelm. This especially appeals to professionals who need to stay informed but don't have the time for extensive reading.

Paid newsletters also serve as educational platforms, providing step-by-step guides, tutorials, or even mini-courses that help subscribers build new skills or deepen their knowledge. I have subscribed to newsletters that offer practical tutorials. Some offer bite-sized lessons on improving writing craft, with practical exercises in every issue. This turns the newsletter into an ongoing learning resource, offering immense value for those wanting to improve their skills.

One of my friends runs a paid newsletter that provides mini-courses in creative writing, broken down into weekly lessons. Subscribers love it because they are not just reading passive content. They are actively learning and growing over time. These newsletters are valuable for anyone looking to gain a new skill without committing to a formal class.

Some newsletters focus on providing detailed how-to guides in specific fields, from business to personal development. For instance, I've written educational pieces that teach professionals how to improve their content marketing strategy, making the newsletter a useful tool they can revisit regularly.

8. Support for Independent Creators & Community Engagement

FINALLY, SOME SUBSCRIBERS connect with independent creators on a personal level, appreciating the insights, challenges, and stories shared in newsletters. They are not just paying for content — they're supporting a creator's journey.

These types of subscribers love authentic, behind-the-scenes insights. For example, a friend's newsletter shares her experiences as a freelance writer, and her readers value the transparency and the personal connection they build with her. Personal stories and reflections make the content more relatable and human. I have shared my own career transitions in newsletters, and subscribers feel more connected when I open up about my journey.

They subscribe to directly support independent creators. Unlike large media outlets, these creators rely on subscriber funding to produce valuable content. For instance, readers have told me they subscribe to help sustain my writing career.

Paid newsletters enable community through interactive features, making subscribers feel more involved and connected. Some newsletters engage readers by polling them on future content topics. This makes subscribers feel valued and gives creators a clear direction based on audience preferences. A colleague in the tech space regularly uses polls to tailor her content to her subscribers' interests.

Hosting live Q&A sessions allows subscribers to engage directly with the creator and get personalized responses. This enhances the content's value and strengthens the bond between the creator and the audience. Some newsletters offer private spaces, like Slack groups, where subscribers can interact with each other and the creator, creating a close-knit community around shared interests.

Part 2: Types of Content Readers Don't Want to Pay For

IN THIS SECTION, I highlight common pitfalls to avoid based on my experience and observations. During my research, I examined the main reasons why readers don't subscribe or cancel paid subscriptions. As they are self-explanatory, I will just list them.

1 — Generic, easily available content from the web

2 — Irrelevant or off-topic content

3 — Overly promotional or sales-focused content

4 — Newsletters with an unclear value proposition

5 — Overwhelming volume of content

6 — Unfinished or underdeveloped ideas

7 — Low-quality or rushed writing

8 — Paying for what was previously free

The last one is a bit tricky because people hesitate to spend money on something they used to get for free. It can feel like a sudden shift in value perception, leading to reluctance or frustration from potential subscribers.

Readers may feel entitled to continue accessing free content, especially if they have followed a creator for a long time. It can be difficult for them to see the added value in paying for something that was once free.

There is an abundance of free content online, making it harder to convince readers to pay when they can easily find other options. Subscribers must trust that the paid content will truly be worth their money and offer something new or superior.

To overcome this challenge, it is important to define the value clearly. Giving potential subscribers a taste of what they will get for their money through a free trial or sample can ease them into the idea of paying. We can emphasize the specific perks of subscribing, such as direct access to the creator, exclusive community features, or premium resources that aren't available elsewhere.

To rule out the first seven points, you can ask these questions yourself:

1 — IS MY CONTENT UNIQUE, OR IS IT SOMETHING READERS CAN EASILY FIND ELSEWHERE ONLINE?

2 — IS MY CONTENT RELEVANT AND ENGAGING FOR MY TARGET AUDIENCE?

3 — AM I FOCUSING TOO MUCH ON SALES AND SELF-PROMOTION, OR PROVIDING REAL VALUE?

4 — DOES MY NEWSLETTER HAVE A CLEAR PURPOSE AND DELIVER MEANINGFUL VALUE TO READERS?

5 — IS MY CONTENT CONCISE, OR DOES IT OVERWHELM MY AUDIENCE WITH UNNECESSARY DETAILS?

6 — ARE MY IDEAS WELL-DEVELOPED AND VALUABLE FOR MY READERS?

7 — AM I CONSISTENTLY PRODUCING HIGH-QUALITY CONTENT WITHOUT RUSHING TO PUBLISH?

Here is a reality check for beginners.

How Ted's Return to 9-to-5 Made Him Happier After an Online Writing Business Failure[1]

<u>Discover Why Going Back To Corporate Life Made This Person Happier And Wiser And The Key Lessons Aspiring Content...[2]</u>

Conclusions and Key Takeaways

UNDERSTANDING WHY READERS are willing to pay for Substack newsletters and why content fails to attract subscribers is essential for aspiring writers.

The insights I gathered from successful creators and extensive research reveal that subscribers are drawn to content that offers exclusivity, depth, and unique perspectives. High-quality, expert-driven, and niche content that provides real value and engages readers on a personal level can justify a subscription fee and encourage a loyal following. Interaction and community spirit are also key conversion factors.

Conversely, content that is generic, overly promotional, or lacks clear value can deter potential subscribers. Readers are reluctant to pay for material that they can easily find elsewhere for free, or that overwhelms them with irrelevant information. Ensuring that your content is well-developed, focused, and delivers on its promise is key to maintaining and growing your subscriber base.

One key point for subscriber satisfaction is regular publishing. It is important because readers get frustrated when they pay for an inconsistent newsletter. I once subscribed to a newsletter that promised weekly insights, but the creator often skipped weeks or sent content sporadically. This lack of consistency made me lose trust in the value of the subscription, and I eventually cancelled. Subscribers want reliability; if the content isn't delivered as promised, they may feel shortchanged.

By thoughtfully addressing these aspects, we can craft a newsletter that attracts paying subscribers and builds a meaningful connection with our audience. We need to emphasize the unique value of our content, avoid common pitfalls, and continuously refine our approach to offer something that truly stands out in a crowded market.

---

1. https://medium.com/illumination/how-teds-return-to-9-to-5-made-him-happier-after-an-online-writing-business-failure-fe56fd60a8f5

2. https://medium.com/illumination/how-teds-return-to-9-to-5-made-him-happier-after-an-online-writing-business-failure-fe56fd60a8f5

Related to this story from a conversion point of view, you may also check out my monthly progress on eight different platforms in August 2024 as a content developer and marketer, which might surprise you.

An In-Depth Performance Review of 8 Major Platforms I Contributed to This Month: Key Insights and...[3]

Discover an independent and comprehensive analysis of my contributions and performance across multiple platforms...[4]

3.   https://medium.com/illumination/an-in-depth-performance-review-of-8-major-platforms-i-contributed-to-this-month-key-insights-and-be5443f86112

4.   https://medium.com/illumination/an-in-depth-performance-review-of-8-major-platforms-i-contributed-to-this-month-key-insights-and-be5443f86112

Chapter 9: How Do the BOOST Options Work on Substack, and How Will I Supplement It With Community Power?

In this chapter, I will guide you through the power of Substack's Boost feature. Specifically tailored for newsletter creators — especially freelance writers — it is a tool designed to help you gain visibility, grow your subscriber base, and, most importantly, convert free readers into paying subscribers.

Substack said[1] "Boost is our most comprehensive investment to date in helping writers accelerate their businesses. For writers who opt into Boost, we'll work in the background to optimize your revenue by determining the most opportune times to offer a particular subscriber a special offer, including free trials, discounts on paid subscriptions, gift subscriptions, or the like. For example, we may use Boost to optimize free-to-paidconversion on promotional surfaces and to help prevent subscribers from churning. These upsell efforts require no time from the writer to manage or implement – and you can opt-outat any time."

Why and How to Configure Boost Options on Substack Newsletters

YOU CAN ACCESS THE boost options from the settings page of your newsletter, as shown in the following screenshot. I will break down five individual features with relatable examples and best practices for freelance writers.

---

1.   https://support.substack.com/hc/en-us/articles/9674586580244-What-is-Substack-Boost

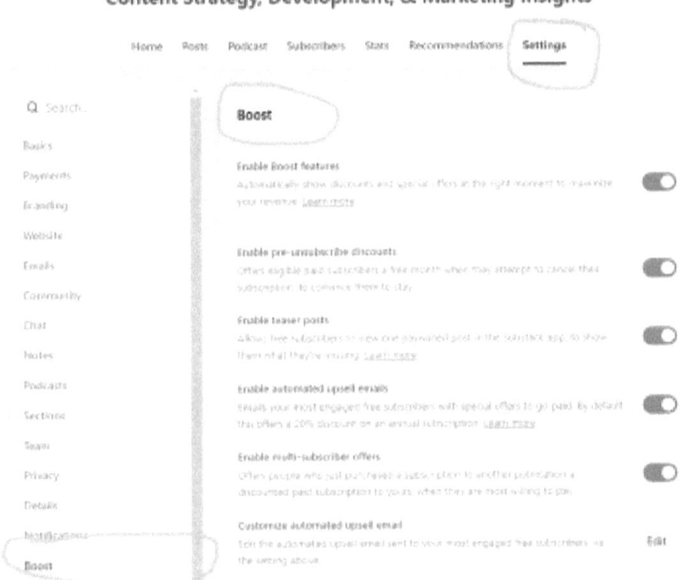

First, you need to enable the Boost features, and then you can learn about the rest and choose the ones that suit your strategy, plans, goals, and aspirations.

1 — Enable Pre-Unsubscribe Discounts

THIS OPTION OFFERS eligible paid subscribers a free month when they attempt to cancel their subscription.

Imagine a subscriber is about to cancel after their first paid month. Before they leave, Substack offers them a free month to convince them to stay. This gives you another opportunity to re-engage them with compelling content.

You can use this as a retention tool by publishing your most valuable and engaging content during that free month. For example, if your newsletter covers freelance writing tips, ensure the next issue offers actionable advice on how writers can land high-paying clients.

2 — Enable Teaser Posts

THIS OPTION ALLOWS free subscribers to view one paywalled post in the Substack app to entice them to pay.

Let's say you have published an enticing paid post. Teaser posts allow free subscribers to read this high-value content and give them a taste of what they are missing.

For this teaser feature, you can choose one of your most compelling posts—something that offers immense value, like solving a pressing problem for your target audience. Teaser posts should intrigue your readers and motivate them to unlock the full experience by subscribing.

3 — Enable Automated Upsell Emails

THIS OPTION SENDS AUTOMATED emails to your most engaged free subscribers with special offers (by default, a 20% discount on an annual subscription).

If a reader regularly opens and reads your free content but hasn't yet paid for a subscription, Substack will automatically send them a personalized email offering a discount to go paid.

You can customize these emails to reflect your tone and the value of your newsletter. You can emphasize the benefits of subscribing, such as exclusive tips, behind-the-scenes content, or personal Q&A sessions. You need to make it clear why upgrading to a paid plan will enhance their experience.

4 — Enable Multi-Subscriber Offers

THIS OPTION PROVIDES people who just purchased a subscription to another Substack publication a discounted paid subscription to yours.

If a reader has just subscribed to another Substack on similar topics, they will be offered a discounted subscription to your newsletter. This feature taps into the reader's willingness to invest more when they have just committed to a purchase.

You can create alliances with other writers who cover related or complementary topics. For example, if you focus on writing tips, partner with a newsletter that covers editing or marketing for freelancers. This helps you capture subscribers already primed to pay for content in your niche.

5 — Customize Automated Upsell Email

THIS OPTION ALLOWS you to edit the automated upsell emails sent to your most engaged free subscribers.

Rather than sending a generic upsell email, you can craft a more personalized message highlighting why your content is worth paying for. For instance, if your newsletter focuses on freelance writing tips, you can mention how the paid version provides in-depth guides on pitching, networking, and scaling a freelance business.

You can use language that feels personal and approachable. Highlight paid subscribers' exclusive benefits, such as deeper insights, access to premium resources, or community interactions. You could also use urgency tactics, like limited-time offers, to encourage quicker conversions.

As you can see, I turned all options to get benefits from each of them.

Boost

Enable Boost features
Automatically show discounts and special offers at the right moment to maximize your revenue. Learn more

Enable pre-unsubscribe discounts
Offers eligible paid subscribers a free month when they attempt to cancel their subscription, to convince them to stay.

Enable teaser posts
Allows free subscribers to view one paywalled post in the Substack app, to show them what they're missing. Learn more

Enable automated upsell emails
Emails your most engaged free subscribers with special offers to go paid. By default this offers a 20% discount on an annual subscription. Learn more

Enable multi-subscriber offers
Offers people who just purchased a subscription to another publication a discounted paid subscription to yours, when they are most willing to pay.

Customize automated upsell email
Edit the automated upsell email sent to your most engaged free subscribers via the setting above.

Edit

Best Practices for Freelancers to Maximize Boost Features of

Substack Newsletters

BASED ON MY INTERVIEWS with the best-selling Substack writers, I distil my findings into the following key points that might give you some valuable insights for your boost strategy.

Focus on Value and Exclusivity: When using teaser posts or automated upsell emails, always emphasize the exclusive content, resources, or insider knowledge paid subscribers will get. Freelancers often have niche expertise, so leverage that to make your audience feel like they're getting special insider access.

Create High-Converting Content: Use your most popular and impactful content for teaser posts. This will give free subscribers a clear reason to upgrade because they'll see firsthand what they're missing out on.

Leverage Discounts at Key Moments: Timing is crucial. The Boost feature helps you automatically offer discounts at the right moments, like when readers try to unsubscribe or after they've engaged with multiple free posts. Readers are most likely to reconsider and stay on or convert in these moments.

Personalize Your Upsell Approach: Don't treat all subscribers the same. Use the customization feature to edit upsell emails with tailored messages that resonate with your audience's needs and aspirations. Show how subscribing will help them grow or solve their biggest problems.

Collaborate with Other Writers: Use the multi-subscriber offer to partner with other writers. Reach out to newsletters that cover similar or complementary topics and offer mutual discounts to each other's subscribers, creating a win-win situation.

I designed a supplementary Boost program for our Substack Mastery community.

AS A COMMUNITY LEADER, I created a supplementary Boost program tailored specifically for our Substack Mastery community. While Substack's automated features are impressive, this program takes things further, enhancing the value members gain from our collective efforts.

Our community currently boasts over 100K subscribers — primarily free — but we are proud to have 112 founding members and several hundred freelance subscribers, all with substantial followings. Together, we are building a content ecosystem **through my website** [2]where writers thrive and audiences grow.

The primary goals of my supplementary Boost program include:

- **Increased Visibility and Reach:** Elevating your content to a broader audience through strategic exposure.
- **Enhanced Credibility:** Building trust and authority as your work gains recognition across networks.
- **SEO and Social Media Boost:** Maximizing discoverability through targeted optimization, ensuring your content ranks higher and gains more engagement.
- **Personal Branding:** Strengthening your unique voice and positioning yourself as a thought leader in your niche.
- **Paid Subscriber Conversions:** Turning free subscribers into loyal paying readers, ultimately driving revenue growth.

This Special Boost Program is designed to be a powerful engine for growth, giving writers the tools to build a lasting audience and expand their authority — not just on Substack but across multiple platforms.

Whether you are a seasoned freelancer or a content entrepreneur, this program can help you transform your writing into a sustainable business.

Let me introduce the essential items in my draft design and discuss the benefits.

1 — Curated Guest Post Per Month with a Guest Author Profile

FEATURING A CURATED guest post each month is a smart move for any writer looking to break into new audiences. You instantly boost your visibility and credibility by showcasing your work to a fresh, engaged community.

Plus, by adding your profile as a guest author, you are not just getting a one-time feature — you are building your SEO value and leaving a digital footprint that drives traffic back to your own Substack or website.

---

2.   https://digitalmehmet.com/illumination-substack-community-support/

Imagine being a freelance writer with valuable tips to share. Through this guest post opportunity, you offer advice to thousands of eager readers and position yourself as an expert in the field.

This kind of exposure is invaluable, helping you grow your audience and expand your reach far beyond your existing circle. It is a win-win that every serious content creator should take advantage of.

2 — Interview Story from My Substack Account with Top 10 Substack Posts of the Writer

BEING INTERVIEWED BY a fellow writer/editor like me provides you with personal and professional exposure. Highlighting the top 10 Substack posts can add to the writer's credibility and showcase their best work, potentially converting readers into loyal followers or paying subscribers.

For example, if a writer is a business coach, the interview can highlight their journey and top posts, offering the audience practical business advice while promoting the writer's expertise.

Here are 3 sample interviews I posted to my **Content Strategy, Development, & Marketing Insights**[3] newsletter on Substack, subscribed by over 28,500 readers, each receiving over 100K views amplified by **my website**[4] and social media accounts like LinkedIn, which I covered **in a previous chapter**[5] of Substack Mastery titled:

"How to Increase Paid Subscribers Case Study #1: Social media is good for promoting Substack, but nothing can beat LinkedIn in converting free subscribers to paid ones based on my experience"

This one is for **Veronica Llorca-Smith**[6], a Substack best-selling author.

<u>Interview with Veronica Llorca-Smith to Inspire Substack Writers</u>[7]

<u>Lovely Veronica Is a Bestselling Substack Creator, Professional Speaker, Award-Winning Author, Ironman Triathlete...</u>**drmehmetyildiz.substack.com**[8]

---

3.   https://drmehmetyildiz.substack.com/

4.   https://digitalmehmet.com

5.   https://medium.com/illumination/substack-mastery-book-chapter-7-dd5f6752aac0

6.   https://medium.com/u/77698eaeabab

7.   https://drmehmetyildiz.substack.com/p/interview-with-veronica-llorca-smith

This one is for our legendary Tim Denning, who is also a Substack best-selling author with a billion content views across multiple platforms.

Why Did I Interview My Aussie Friend Tim Denning Again on Medium & Substack?[9]

This highly followed writer, known for their viral content on Medium, is now getting 50 times more views on Substack...**drmehmetyildiz.substack.com**[10]

This one is for **Wendi Gordon**[11] a seasoned freelance writer, a community builder, who has remarkable contributions to the mental health field via various content sites.

Episode 1: Interview with Wendi Gordon[12]

Freelance writer, book author, mental health champion, and former pastor with a social worker and master of divinity...[13]

3 — One Well-Crafted Post with Annotation and a Photo of the Author Per Month

THE ANNOTATION IN THE post adds personalized commentary, enriching the content and creating a more engaging experience for readers.

The photo humanizes the content, making it more relatable and memorable. This increases the reader's connection with the writer, leading to stronger engagement.

Annotating a post about productivity with a real-life example from the author's journey adds depth, making the advice more actionable for readers.

---

8. https://drmehmetyildiz.substack.com/p/interview-with-veronica-llorca-smith

9. **https://drmehmetyildiz.substack.com/p/why-did-i-interview-my-aussie-friend**

10. https://drmehmetyildiz.substack.com/p/why-did-i-interview-my-aussie-friend

11. **https://medium.com/u/26c6c4b14c1d**

12. **https://drmehmetyildiz.substack.com/p/episode-1-interview-with-wendi-gordon**

13. https://drmehmetyildiz.substack.com/p/episode-1-interview-with-wendi-gordon

4 — One Weekly Special Social Media Post with Top 3 Stories and Preferred Images of Writers on Multiple Platforms

POSTING ACROSS PLATFORMS like LinkedIn, X Premium, Quora, Facebook, Typepad, and Reddit enables the writer to reach diverse audiences, significantly boosting visibility.

Highlighting their top stories and images **on tailored social media platforms** can enhance branding and content recognition.

Freelance writers could promote their content strategy stories on a specific platform while showcasing their creative process on multiple other platforms, reaching different segments of potential clients or followers.

5 — One Special Blog Post Per Month with Key Achievements, Top 10 Posts, and Intellectual Properties

SHOWCASING KEY ACHIEVEMENTS and top posts positions the freelance writers as thought leaders.

Highlighting intellectual properties like eBooks, training programs, or mentoring guides can lead to sales and further credibility while summarizing these in a blog post solidifies the writer's reputation and attracts more subscribers or clients.

For an author who has launched a course on digital marketing, featuring their achievements and posts can drive new traffic and help them sell their course or attract new consultancy clients.

All ethical and authentic writers are welcome **to join my community**[14].

By thoughtfully managing the boost aspects, we can craft a newsletter that attracts paying subscribers and builds a meaningful connection with our audience. We need to emphasize the unique value of our content, avoid common pitfalls, and continuously refine our approach to offer something that truly stands out in a crowded market.

---

14.   https://digitalmehmet.com/illumination-substack-community-support/

Chapter 10: How to Use Substack Newsletters for Marketing and Sales for Supplementary Income

One of the most common questions I receive is whether freelance writers can use Substack to market and sell their products or services and how to do it effectively. The short answer is yes, but it is crucial to understand the process, its nuances, best practices, and pitfalls, as I will cover in this chapter since most readers are turned off by overt marketing or sales content. I created this chapter after interviewing some best-selling Substack writers and observing their behaviour by subscribing to their content.

In the grand scheme, everyone is engaged in selling something — whether it is their time, ideas, products, or services. For instance, Medium offers free services but monetizes through memberships, Substack facilitates creators' newsletters and earns a 10% commission, and Google profits from advertisements. As creators, we should embrace this reality and not be intimidated by offering our ideas, supplementary services, or products, as it is a natural and essential part of the ecosystem.

While I sell my ideas in my stories or newsletters, I do not directly sell products or services as they are not my main goals. However, in line with best practices followed by many writers, readers, professionals, and thought leaders, I include thoughtfully curated links to relevant marketing or sales pages when needed.

This approach ensures that genuinely interested readers can easily find additional resources or services without feeling pressured, enhancing their experience while maintaining the integrity and value of the content. It strikes a balance between offering valuable information and providing opportunities for further engagement, allowing readers to explore at their own pace.

The key to success on Substack is building a loyal audience before attempting any marketing or sales activities. This starts with consistently delivering high-quality content that engages and delights your readers. By focusing on free yet high-value content — like life lessons, expert tips, guides, or tutorials — you can establish trust and encourage readers to comment, share, and subscribe to your newsletter.

Once you have built an audience, the next step is converting free subscribers into paying ones, a process I have covered extensively in the previous chapter titled **"Why Readers Pay for Substack Newsletters and What Type of Content Fails to Attract Subscribers[1]."**

While this transition takes time and effort, having paid subscribers makes marketing much easier. However, even at this stage, handling direct sales with care is necessary. If readers feel like they are being sold to instead of informed or inspired, they may unsubscribe.

Best-selling newsletters include a call to action (CTA) at the end of each edition. The CTA offers valuable, informative content first, then subtly suggests products or services. For example, a CTA might invite readers to hire you for a writing project or consult with you on a specific topic.

Many successful freelance writers also sell digital products — like eBooks, templates, courses, or guides — through their Substack. One example I've come across is an SEO writer who sold an eBook on mastering SEO copywriting after first sharing techniques and personal experiences in their newsletter. Similarly, freelancers often host paid webinars or workshops. For instance, a grant writer I know offers paid sessions teaching others how to write successful grant proposals.

Another income stream freelance writers can explore is affiliate marketing, where you recommend products you use or believe in. It is a legitimate and common business practice. As I documented before **Affiliate Marketing Can Enhance Writers' Lifestyle[2]**. I have written a book on this topic titled **The Power of Digital Affiliate Marketing[3]**, so you can find best practices in it.

---

1.   https://medium.com/illumination/substack-mastery-book-chapter-8-9939d5939493

2.   https://medium.com/illumination/this-passive-income-skill-can-enhance-writers-lifestyle-e58347f3139e

Additionally, **Substack's referral program**[4] is an effective way to grow your subscriber base by encouraging current readers to refer others, often incentivized with free content or discounts.

Some of my mentors use their Substack as a **portfolio hub,** a centralized online space where professionals share details about their work, skills, and achievements to attract potential clients or employers. They don't push readers to buy but make purchase options available for those interested. They add links to products and services in the newsletter's signature.

Finally, I have noticed that many newsletters offer one-on-one coaching sessions, tutorials, or career guidance in their CTA section. These subtle but impactful offers at the end of a newsletter can be a highly effective way to generate income without alienating your readers.

Related to sales and marketing sales, one of the common questions is about sponsored posts. Handling sponsored posts as a freelance writer requires a delicate balance between providing value to your audience and fulfilling the sponsor's expectations.

First and foremost, transparency is key. We must clearly disclose the sponsorship to maintain trust with our readers. Ensure the content aligns with your personal brand and audience's interests, blending seamlessly with your usual style.

The sponsored content should provide genuine value, offering helpful insights, tips, information, or inspiration rather than coming across as a blatant advertisement.

Therefore, we can focus on storytelling that highlights the sponsor's product or service in a relatable and authentic way that resonates with our readers. To benefit from sponsored posts, it is important to negotiate fair compensation that reflects the effort and reach of your newsletter while adhering to the editorial and curation standards.

By following these principles — building trust first, offering value, and approaching sales with a light touch — you can use Substack not just as a platform for writing but as a powerful tool for marketing and selling your products or services.

---

3.   https://medium.com/illumination-book-chapters/the-power-of-digital-affiliate-marketing-chapter-1-95968b0bf2e9

4.   https://on.substack.com/p/subscriber-referrals

Links to Available Chapters of Substack Mastery Book

PREFACE OF "SUBSTACK Mastery" for Beta Readers[5], Chapter 1[6], Chapter 2[7], Chapter 3[8], Chapter 4[9], Chapter 5[10], Chapter 6[11], Chapter 7[12], Chapter 8[13], Chapter 9[14], Chapter 10[15], Chapter 11[16], Chapter 12[17], Chapter 13[18], Chapter 14[19], Chapter 15[20], Chapter 16[21], Chapter 17[22], Chapter 18[23], Chapter 19[24]...

Summary of Best Practices for Marketing and Sales

AS CREATORS, IT IS essential to master marketing and sales. However, we must understand that readers subscribe to newsletters for information, education, inspiration, and entertainment. Marketing and sales should always remain secondary and carefully balanced to avoid overshadowing the primary purpose of your content.

---

5. https://medium.com/illumination/the-first-chapter-of-my-new-book-substack-mastery-for-beta-readers-2d0e4fa86e78

6. https://medium.com/illumination/substack-mastery-book-chapter-1-cb3104341985

7. https://medium.com/illumination/substack-mastery-book-chapter-2-d1b28edab420

8. https://medium.com/illumination/substack-mastery-book-chapter-3-e13b575f1598

9. https://medium.com/illumination/substack-mastery-book-chapter-4-f5829191e7ae

10. https://medium.com/illumination/substack-mastery-book-chapter-5-3e84cc43b4be

11. https://medium.com/illumination/substack-mastery-book-chapter-6-e65ae83264ee

12. https://medium.com/illumination/substack-mastery-book-chapter-7-dd5f6752aac0

13. https://medium.com/illumination/substack-mastery-book-chapter-8-9939d5939493

14. https://medium.com/illumination-curated/substack-mastery-book-chapter-9-2ac3c36c3ee7

15. https://medium.com/illumination/substack-mastery-book-chapter-10-a1ad6e9bd4bd

16. https://medium.com/illumination/substack-mastery-book-chapter-11-364110cbf957

17. https://medium.com/illumination/substack-mastery-book-chapter-12-86b59a784fd4

18. https://medium.com/illumination/substack-mastery-book-chapter-13-1bdde6628dea

19. https://dr-mehmet-yildiz.medium.com/substack-mastery-book-chapter-14-039eda9b2102

20. https://medium.com/illumination/substack-mastery-book-chapter-15-6dce1c6b820b

21. https://medium.com/illumination/substack-mastery-book-chapter-16-eebfab51abdb

22. https://medium.com/illumination/substack-mastery-book-chapter-17-aea5f848509b

23. https://medium.com/illumination/substack-mastery-book-chapter-18-a-special-chapter-for-book-authors-fbd54e900906

24. https://www.patreon.com/posts/
14-powerful-to-112816055?utm_medium=clipboard_copy&utm_source=copyLink&utm_campaign=postshare_fan&utm_content=web_share

Based on my interactions and observations with some of the best-selling Substack writers, I have distilled the following principles, which you can adapt to your own needs, goals, and aspirations:

1. **Produce high-quality content consistently** that is informative, engaging, and relevant. Establishing trust through great content is key to converting readers into paying customers.
2. **Know your audience** before crafting your marketing strategy. Understand their needs, pain points, and interests. Tailor your content and offerings to resonate deeply with them.
3. **Focus on building long-term relationships** rather than pushing for a quick sale. Engage with your readers through comments, replies, and social media interactions to build rapport.
4. **Educate and provide value first.** Focus on solving your audience's problems and building relationships. Let them come to you for solutions rather than overwhelming them with sales pitches.
5. **Build credibility with testimonials and case studies.** Include reviews from satisfied customers or showcase successful projects to highlight your value. Display these testimonials in your newsletters or on sales pages to boost trust.
6. **Maintain a consistent tone, style, and message** across all your marketing materials. A coherent brand strengthens your reputation and helps your audience know what to expect from you.
7. **Optimize your content for SEO** to improve visibility on search engines. Use relevant keywords in titles, headings, and content. Promote your newsletter on social media, using hashtags on platforms like Twitter, Facebook, LinkedIn, Quora, or Reddit for increased reach.
8. **Research industry standards** and price your services based on the value you provide. Knowing what the market is charging ensures your pricing is competitive and fair.
9. **Offer different pricing tiers** for your products or services. This allows you to cater to both casual readers and those seeking premium offerings.
10. **Create urgency** with limited-time promotions or discounts. If done

with integrity, this strategy can encourage conversions without being pushy. Common tactics include "limited-time offer" or "discount available until [date]."

11. **Test different strategies.** Experiment with messaging, calls-to-action (CTAs), and platforms. A/B testing allows you to compare what works best. Regularly review analytics to understand which content resonates, how long readers engage, and what drives conversions.

12. **Diversify your channels** and repurpose content. Don't rely solely on one platform or marketing channel. Spread your presence across multiple outlets, such as Substack, Medium, your own website, and social media, to reach a broader audience.

By following these best practices, you can effectively market your products and services while maintaining the integrity of your content, building lasting relationships with your audience, and ultimately achieving long-term success for your main writing business and side hustles.

Summary of Common Pitfalls to Avoid

WHILE MARKETING AND selling through your Substack newsletter can be highly effective, several common mistakes can undermine your efforts. By avoiding these pitfalls, you can maintain the trust of your audience and increase the chances of long-term success:

1. **Pushing for a sale too soon or too often** without first providing value can alienate your audience. Readers come for information, education, and inspiration—not a hard sell. If your content feels too sales-oriented, you risk losing their trust.

2. **Sticking to one marketing strategy** without experimenting or testing different approaches can delay growth. The online content landscape is constantly changing, and what works today may not work tomorrow. Flexibility and adaptation are key.

3. **Making assumptions about your audience** without backing it up with data can lead to ineffective marketing strategies. We need to regularly analyze our audience's behaviour, preferences, and engagement patterns to meet their needs.

4. **Undervaluing your services by offering low prices** to attract customers can have long-term consequences. While it might draw initial attention, it can make it difficult to raise your prices later, and it risks devaluing your skills and expertise.

By avoiding these pitfalls, you can develop a sustainable and successful approach to marketing and sales, boosting trust and loyalty from your audience while growing your writing business and side hustles.

Conclusions and Key Takeaways

WHEN APPROACHED STRATEGICALLY and carefully, using Substack newsletters as a marketing and sales tool for freelance writers can be a powerful supplementary income avenue.

When marketing and selling products or services as a freelance writer or content entrepreneurs, we must follow best practices and avoid pitfalls to achieve success while avoiding common pitfalls.

By focusing on high-quality, engaging content that builds trust with readers, writers can cultivate lasting relationships for effective sales without compromising the integrity of their newsletter.

As demonstrated, subtlety in promoting products or services and ensuring the primary focus remains on providing value is essential for maintaining reader engagement.

Freelance writers can benefit from experimenting with different approaches to find what resonates with their audience while staying informed about market trends and pricing standards.

Regularly testing and analyzing data is crucial to refining marketing strategies and maintaining growth. Additionally, using testimonials and demonstrating expertise through relevant content can boost credibility and trust among readers.

Ultimately, creating a balanced approach that integrates marketing and sales with valuable, insightful content is vital, ensuring that such efforts enhance rather than detract from the overall reader experience.

Thank you for reading my perspectives. I wish you a healthy and happy life.

About the Substack Mastery Book for Review and Purchase

AS **I shared in a previous post,**[25] this book has already hit the top 100 bestseller list in multiple categories in various Amazon marketplaces. Thank you, my loyal readers, for making this book a success and a valuable knowledge source for the community.

Many thanks to beta readers who started leaving honest feedback on this evolving book **on Goodreads t**[26]oday. If you enjoy and benefit from this book, I'd appreciate leaving honest feedback on Goodreads, as the Amazon version is not ready for review yet.

If you want to purchase the book at a reasonable price or gift it to someone you care about, you may preorder it **via various Amazon markets.**[27] If the editing process is complete on time, I can get it published faster.

The funds generated from this book will be donated to the management of **the Substack Mastery site for the ILLUMINATION community.**[28] This education site also amplifies the newsletters of freelance writers.

---

25. https://medium.com/illumination/how-my-unpublished-book-hit-the-best-seller-rank-in-global-marketing-topic-in-5-days-ef227afe8518

26. https://www.goodreads.com/book/show/218008495-substack-mastery?from_search=true&from_srp=true&qid=c6agMQ7SgI&rank=2

27. https://www.amazon.com/dp/B0DF2K6VNX?ref_=pe_93986420_775043100

28. https://illuminationcurators.substack.com/

Chapter 11: Supercharge Your Substack Newsletters with Blogging on WordPress, Medium, or Other Platforms: Here's What You Need to Know and How to Get Started Right Now

Can Blogging Boost Your Newsletter Growth?

I wrote this chapter because I gained significant benefits from blogging, especially within the last 12 months when I started intensifying my efforts on Substack. Until I deliberately blogged my content published on Substack or sent it through emails, subscriber growth was slow. It was only through limited discovery with the platform's built-in tools.

I have known the importance of blogging since its start, but I wish I had noticed its importance for Substack earlier. I want to highlight this because since I started blogging my Substack posts on my website and guest blogging places, I have noticed significant growth in my three publications on Substack. I own multiple blogs **like this one**[1], contribute as a guest blogger to other blogs, and also invite **guest bloggers to my website**[2], which hosts multiple blogs.

As I highlighted before, I treat Substack as another platform. It cannot replace our own site as we never know its future. They might change the rules or even close the company. Although blogging is possible on Substack, it is not as powerful as an actual blogging platform.

---

1. https://digitalmehmet.com/author/myildiz/

2. https://digitalmehmet.com/blog-posts/

Some writers asked me whether they could use Substack as their sole blogging platform. If you don't have any other option, yes, but Substack is not designed as a major blogging platform as it lacks key blogging features like search engine optimization (SEO) and discovery customization. Thus, from my observations, the discoverability of Substack blogs in search engines is relatively low.

However, Substack positions itself as a blogging service with an email subscription facility, providing some great examples **in this official document**[3]. So, as good news, I assume the company will invest in this program as they do in their subscription services always supporting creators in innovative ways.

I have been investigating blogging platforms for a long time to provide insights to my clients, students, and proteges. Blogging platforms keep changing; some are growing, and some are declining. Finding a good blogging platform can be a good investment for your content marketing strategy.

To give you an example, according to **Forbes**[4], the top seven blogging sites in 2024 are WordPress, Wix, Weebly, Drupal, Squarespace, CMS Hub, and our good old Medium, where I share this story. As you may know, Medium is free and open to the public for blogging, in addition to its partner program, which allows writers to monetize their content.

I have been using WordPress to host my website and Medium as a secondary blogging platform for the last five years. As I introduce **on my site**[5], WordPress.com has many additional tools like Jetpack, Pressable, WooCommerce Marketplace, Akismet, SenseiLMS , and WPJobManager to help me grow my website.

So, I can endorse the effectiveness of both WordPress and Medium for bloggers and freelance writers. For example, both platforms have a domain authority of 95, and many of my posts from these two platforms gained significant visibility, and some even went viral.

Combining WordPress with Medium has been my best content distribution and marketing strategy. Based on my research, these platforms have close to a billion backlinks, which I will cover in another story to highlight the

---

3.   https://substack.com/for-bloggers

4.   https://www.forbes.com/advisor/au/business/software/best-blogging-platforms/

5.   https://digitalmehmet.com/selected-and-recommended-products/

importance of linking domains to increase SEO. Now, adding Substack to the equation can be a game-changer for freelance writers.

You may wonder what blogging on our websites or being a guest blogger on other sites can add to your Substack's growth with compelling reasons. I will explain why blogging is essential for your Substack success, offer best practices to maximize growth and discuss potential pitfalls to avoid.

Consider Substack taking a road trip while blogging, which is like flying. Both help you reach a broad audience, but blogging gets you there faster when you want to promote your own content.

Substack has a built-in boost feature that helps with visibility, as I mentioned in a previous chapter, but if you want to amplify your reach and grow your audience, blogging is a powerful tool. That's why I have added guest blogging **as a complementary boost service for my writing community**[6]. It is the quickest way to give your content a boost.

Now, based on my experience and observations of successful bloggers, I want to highlight some key points about what blogging can do for your content and how it can help you grow your Substack newsletters with notable benefits.

How Blogging Boosts Your Newsletter Growth

BLOGGING HAS A LONG history and can be a powerful tool for freelance writers aiming to succeed on Substack as well. Blogging platforms are geared to allow writers to build an audience, convert readers into paying subscribers, and monetize their content in various ways.

From my experience, blogging on your own website or guest blogging on other sites can significantly contribute to your Substack newsletter growth in various ways. I want to highlight some compelling reasons for considering this strategy.

Posting regularly on your website can increase your online presence and visibility thanks to the focus of search engines that prioritize blog posts.

Readers visiting your blog can discover your Substack newsletter through prominent call-to-actions (like opt-in forms, subscribe buttons, or banners) and subscribe directly via links to newsletters.

---

6.   https://medium.com/p/039d29a28f65

When you guest blog on high-traffic sites relevant to your niche, you expose your content to new audiences. In your blog posts, you can include links to your Substack in the author bio or within the article to drive traffic back to your Substack and convert it into subscribers.

SEO (search engine optimization) is a critical success factor for bloggers and all other content developers. You need to learn the basics. I will cover SEO in another chapter with details and practical tips.

In the meantime, you need to understand that regularly publishing keyword-rich content logically and meaningfully on your own blog can help build domain authority, which can rank your site higher in search results and attract organic traffic. By linking back to your Substack, you increase the chances of converting this traffic into newsletter subscribers.

Writing guest posts for established websites can provide backlinks to your blogging site and Substack newsletters. These backlinks can improve your site's SEO, making it more discoverable on search engines.

Blogging on your website helps establish you as an authority in your niche or expertise areas. Readers who find value in your blog posts are more likely to view your Substack as a credible source of valuable content and subscribe to it.

Being featured as a guest blogger on reputable sites can enhance your credibility and reputation. Readers are more likely to trust and subscribe to your Substack newsletters when they see your expertise acknowledged by established platforms.

Repurposing and diversifying your content is essential for growing your Substack newsletters and your freelance writing business. You can repurpose or expand content from your website or guest blogs into more in-depth pieces for your Substack.

Blogging can keep your Substack content fresh and engaging while also enticing blog readers to subscribe for exclusive and extended insights through your posts.

Guest blogging provides opportunities for cross-promotion. Some hosts may allow you to promote your Substack newsletter directly, and you can invite their readers to explore exclusive content on Substack.

Readers who engage with your blog posts (through comments or shares) might be willing to subscribe to more personal, behind-the-scenes insights via a newsletter. Engaging with your blog's audience through thoughtful responses might encourage more robust relationships and enable a sense of community that can translate into newsletter subscriptions.

By driving blog readers to your Substack, you can increase the likelihood of building a paid subscriber base on Substack. Exclusive paid content or tiers in your Substack can entice readers who already appreciate your blog content to support you monetarily.

Besides, guest blogging on other platforms can lead to collaborations or further guest appearances, expanding your professional network. This new network can introduce you to new readers and subscribers through word-of-mouth or partnerships.

Blogging allows you to test topics and content formats with your audience. Content that performs well on your website or as a guest post can be refined and expanded for your Substack audience. Additionally, collecting feedback from blog readers can help shape future newsletters, ensuring they align with your audience's interests.

Most importantly, you can monetize your blogging in several ways and use Substack as a supplementary growth and income stream. I will write a detailed story about this, as there are some nuances to consider before monetizing a blog.

By integrating blogging into your overall content strategy, you can establish a solid, flexible, and diverse online presence that funnels interested readers into your Substack ecosystem, growing your readership and engagement.

A holistic approach through blogging on your site and being a guest blogger on reputable sites, combining SEO, networking, content repurposing, and audience interaction, can help you grow your Substack subscriber base effectively.

What is the difference between Substack and WordPress for Bloggers?

MOST OF MY CLIENTS, students, and proteges asked me this question during my workshops or mentoring sessions. So, I thought it is worthwhile to touch on it here to give you a perspective.

The biggest differentiator is that Substack is a company, and WordPress is a technology. To explain this idea to them, I use an analogy to make it easy to understand and memorable.

I see Substack as a restaurant with its own unique menu. You can't get the exact same experience elsewhere because it is a company with a specific setup. But you can take your followers with you if you leave, even though the "menu" (features and tools) might change.

WordPress, on the other hand, is more like an oven that many different restaurants use. If one restaurant closes, you can move to another place with the same oven and keep making your pizza (content) the same way since WordPress is a widely used technology, not a single company.

How to Start Blogging for Absolute Beginners

IN THIS SECTION, I extract a chapter from one of my previous books to give a high-level step-by-step guide for absolute beginners to create a website and start blogging to promote their Substack newsletters.

I originally created this based on my experience with WordPress, which has been #1 for bloggers for many years. Many hosting companies use WordPress as their blogging offer due to its rich features and ease of use.

This guide will give beginners the basic steps to get started with blogging to grow your Substack readership without overwhelming technical jargon.

If you already have a blog and know these steps, you can skip them or share them with someone who might need them.

1. Choose a Website Platform

PICK A BLOGGING PLATFORM that's easy to use for beginners. Two popular options are WordPress (great for customization and control) and Wix (ideal for beginners). Your platform will be the backbone of your site. WordPress is widely recommended because it offers flexibility and control, while Wix is user-friendly. But there are many more, so you may find a platform that suits your needs.

2. Register a Domain Name

CHOOSE A DOMAIN NAME that reflects your brand or newsletter. If you sign up with WordPress, they give you a domain name for free for the first year. Some domain names can be very expensive. You may also buy a domain name from vendors like Namecheap at a reasonable price. Keep it simple, memorable, and aligned with your Substack focus. A custom domain looks professional and helps build brand consistency.

3. Sign Up for Web Hosting

IF USING WORDPRESS.org, you will need hosting (like Bluehost or SiteGround). If using WordPress.com or Wix, hosting is included. Many platforms provide hosting. One of my proteges uses Namecheap, which he found cost-effective as a beginner. Remember that reliable hosting ensures your site stays live and performs well.

4. Set Up Your Website

WORDPRESS CAN BE INSTALLED on your hosting platform. Most hosting services offer 1-click installs). Pick a theme that matches your blog's aesthetics and is responsive and mobile-friendly. You may choose free or premium themes depending on your budget. Remember that your site's design can influence first impressions and user experience.

5. Add Essential Pages

CREATE THESE KEY PAGES to start. The most important one is the homepage to introduce yourself and your content, the page to share your story and what your newsletter covers, the contact page to make it easy for readers to reach you, and the newsletter signup to embed your Substack sign-up form or link to it prominently. These are foundational elements of a professional blog.

6. Install Essential Plugins (for WordPress)

YOAST SEO CAN HELP optimize your blog for search engines. One of the volunteer editors of my publication created **a tutorial about Yoast SEO**[7] for the guest bloggers of my site and posted it to our community channel, **Substack Mastery**[8]. WPForms can make it easy to create forms, such as a newsletter signup. Plugins expand your website's functionality without needing technical knowledge. There are many of them that you can consider as you grow your blogging site.

7. Integrate Your Substack to Your Blogging Site

YOU CAN EMBED YOUR Substack newsletter using your unique signup form on key parts of your website (e.g., sidebar, footer, or a dedicated page). You may also add it as a signature at the end of your blogs. You may add a consent field with a tick box to obtain agreement from your audience to subscribe to your newsletters for free. Remember your blog because you want to drive traffic from your blog to grow your Substack subscribers.

8. Write Your First Blog Post, Promote it, and Maintain It

START WITH AN INTRODUCTORY post about your newsletter's focus and value. Use clear headings, and keep it conversational. Include links back to your Substack where relevant. Introduce yourself and connect with potential readers, leading them to your Substack newsletters.

Share your blog posts on social media, in your Substack newsletter, and through guest blogging on other platforms. Promoting your blog drives traffic to your website and Substack, boosting your audience.

To grow your audience, you need to post regularly on your blog and integrate your Substack on your website. It is also a good idea to promote your latest posts to your newsletter audience. Consistency builds engagement and trust with your readers.

---

7. https://www.youtube.com/watch?v=lqT-zAYmi4g

8. https://www.youtube.com/@illuminationsubstackmastery

What is next?

WHILE YOU IMPROVE YOUR blogging skills, you need to use well-placed CTAs, email segmentation, limited-time offers, and testimonials to encourage free readers to convert to paying subscribers.

Remember to track your analytics to see what works and what doesn't. Refine your strategy over time to ensure you are optimizing for growth and paid conversions.

By mastering the art and science of blogging for Substack with consistent, high-value content and clever conversion tactics, you can grow your audience and turn your newsletter into a sustainable income stream as a freelance writer.

Chapter 12: How to Boost Your Paid Memberships with Special Discounts or Mega Deals on Substack Creatively and Joyfully

Money is important for freelancers and content entrepreneurs. However, this chapter isn't just about increasing your income. It is about finding joy in the freelance journey and creating meaningful connections with your readers as a sustainable lifestyle.

If you are a beginner, in this chapter, you will discover practical and impactful strategies to expand your paid membership on Substack while delighting your audience and encouraging loyalty.

While introducing fundamental techniques for using the Substack system via this book, I also aim to inspire you and contribute to your well-being.

Whether you aim to offer exclusive discounts or launch a founding membership, these proven techniques will help you engage subscribers, inspire commitment, and create lasting value.

By applying these strategies, you can not only boost your income but also cultivate a community of readers who are deeply invested in your work. Substack makes everything easy for creators, so we should benefit from their care and generosity.

Key Strategies I Will Cover in This Chapter:

1. **Create a Special Offer:** Use time-limited discounts to drive quick conversions and attract more subscribers.

2. **Offer Discounts Manually:** Tailor discounts to specific subscribers or groups, giving you full control over who receives them and under what conditions.
3. **Gift Memberships:** Reward loyal subscribers by gifting them a membership, making them feel valued and more connected to your work.
4. **Bundle Memberships:** Sweeten the deal by offering extra perks for founding members, making them feel like VIPs with exclusive access.
5. **Create a Mega Special Deals:** Use a special occasion to reward loyal readers as I did.

The Power of Discounts: A Personal Case Study

ON 1 SEPTEMBER 2024, I received advice from a best-selling Substack author who suggested I offer a special discount for one of my newsletters.

He predicted that a 20% discount could double my paid subscribers — and he was right. In just ten days, my paid subscriptions increased by almost 200%.

Here is the special discount I created and tested from a subscriber account. I called it Substack Mastery Book Celebration after my book hit the best-seller book.

It was an excellent way to celebrate this unexpected success, provided I give my content 100% free for this book until this chapter and will continue to do so.

Here is a graphical view of this publication when I turned on the discount on the first of September.

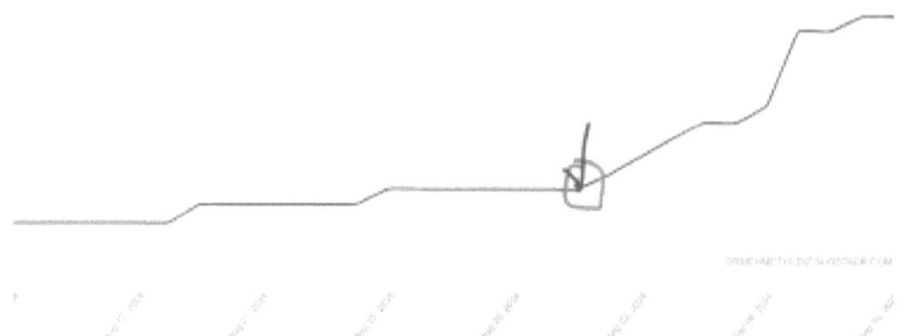

The lesson here? **Discounts work, especially when timed and targeted correctly.**

Step-by-Step Guide to Offering Special Discounts on Substack

YOU CAN ACCESS THE following screenshot through the settings of your publications on Substack.com.

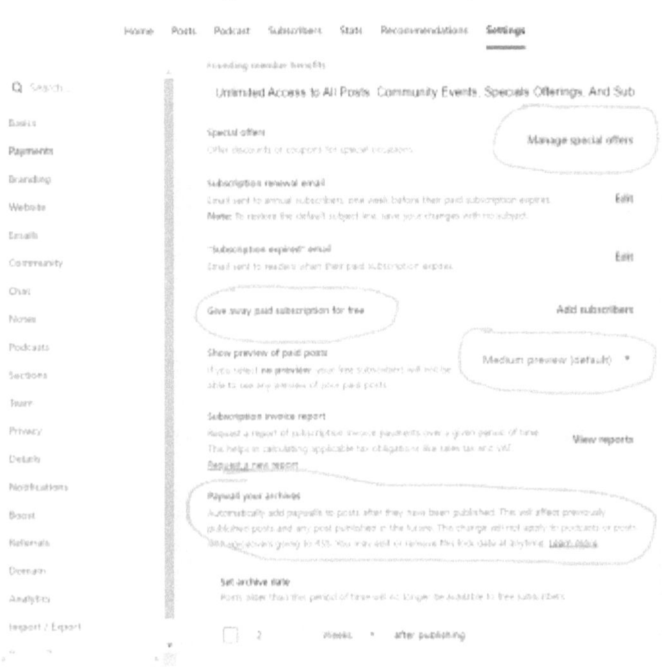

How to Create a Special Offer

- Go to your Substack publication's dashboard.
- Click on "Settings" > "Paid Subscriptions" > "Discounts."
- Create a time-limited discount (e.g., 20% off for one month).
- Promote this offer in your newsletters and on social media.

WHEN YOU COMPLETE IT, you will see this screen with a description, a link, and terms. This is a screenshot from my newsletter settings.

Content Strategy, Development, & Marketing Insights

Home   Posts   Podcast   Subscribers   Stats   Recommendations   Settings

← Back

Substack Mastery Book Celebration   Edit   Delete

https://drmehmetyildiz.substack.com/2ebafc07

Copy link   Send by email

Description
Members who purchased my book or provided feedback as a beta reader

Terms
20% off for 1 year
Only applies to yearly subscriptions

You can copy the link and share it as a CTA on your newsletters, blog posts, articles, or social media. You may also send it directly to your subscribers via email.

How to Offer Discounts Manually

- Select specific subscribers or groups who you think would benefit from a personalized discount.
- Craft a custom email explaining the exclusive offer just for them.
- Use the "Gift" option under "Paid Subscriptions" to apply their discount.

How to Gift Memberships to Loyal Subscribers

- Under "Settings," go to "Subscriptions" and select the "Gift a Subscription" option.
- Choose loyal subscribers or fans you want to reward.
- Send a personalized note explaining why you're gifting them a membership — it adds a thoughtful touch.

Create Mega Discounts for Limited Time Only

- Offer an 80% discount for your founding members (e.g., for a membership priced at $500, they would pay $100). I explain this in the next section as there is a nuance that you need to understand
- Highlight the benefits of being a founding member — exclusive content, early access, or other perks.
- Promote this special offer through your newsletters, making sure your free subscribers know they're getting a rare opportunity.

Why Mega Discounts Matter

FOR THOSE OF YOU WITH a large following, plenty of free subscribers, and some paid members, **mega discounts** — like founding memberships with substantial discounts — can be invaluable.

They drive more paid subscriptions and make your subscribers feel special and appreciated. Offering a "Founding Member" status with exclusive content or perks creates a sense of belonging and rewards their loyalty.

Founding membership for established writers is very important. It is extra important to me because I see founding members as my lifetime business partners to interact and create synergistic effects mutually.

For me, offering a mega discount is particularly important because I don't write to earn income from my writing for a living as I have other better income-generating streams, which I invested **over the last 42 years**[1] while working in the corporate world until retiring in 2021.

I give 90% of content for free and only monetize 10% to donate it to my charity organization to support other content developers and thought leaders who can illuminate society. I encourage them to monetize their content as most of them make their living from content development or marketing.

Founding membership for this publication is $500, as **I provide a comprehensive service for these members.**[2] It is not just posting articles or

---

[1]   https://medium.com/sensible-biohacking-transhumanism/i-wish-i-had-gone-self-employed-40-years-ago-for-three-reasons-7739e5afa150

newsletters. I support freelance writers and content developers, offering them guidance, content boosting, and extended marketing in my network.

To make my founding member tier accessible to a broad audience, I offered a 90% discounted mega deal. This means that by paying just $51 yearly, they can get a value of $500 investment.

I would like to explain how to implement this strategy in your Substack as there is no direct way to do it. When we give a special discount, let's say 20%, it applies to both tiers.

My solution was to leverage a unique tool for the Founding members. Substack allows creators to give an option for this tier. It is not a discount but a bargaining deal.

How I Offered a Mega Discount for Founding Members

THE FOLLOWING SCREENSHOT shows the value of my recent founding membership.

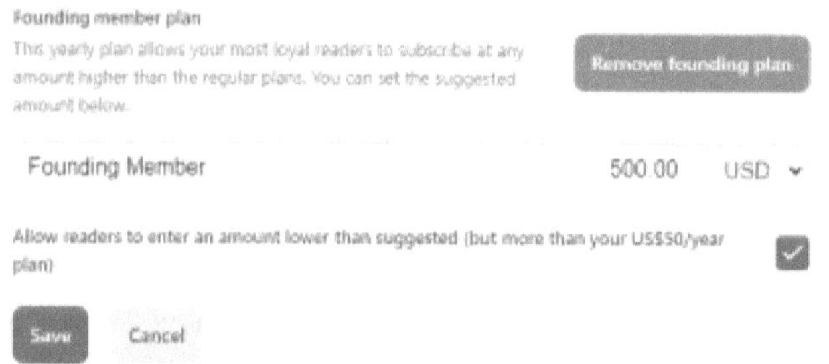

My solution for a mega discount was to check the box that says, '**Allow readers to enter an amount lower than the suggested price.**' This arrangement will allow interested subscribers to upgrade it by paying $51 instead of $500 annually.

This means that for a limited time, only my current subscribers paying already $50 for basic membership will upgrade to founding membership with just an extra $1. I wish I could cut off this $1, but Substack does not allow me to do so for good reasons.

---

2.   https://medium.com/illumination/the-strategic-move-illumination-communitys-commercial-arm-for-charitable-success-039d29a28f65

Why do we need a workaround to achieve such a mega deal?

It is because Substack does not allow membership fees of less than $5 a month. I had to stick with that minimum, which makes sense because Substack needs to earn from creators' income. On our own websites, we can allocate any amount, but on Substack, we cannot.

This is understandable because, unlike platforms like Medium, which charge $5 or $15 in membership fees, Substack gives creators free access to their tools and only earns money when creators start earning. It is a fair model that aligns their success with ours.

I'd like to briefly explain my goals and aspirations as a content developer, marketing strategist, and community builder.

According to my recent review of stats, around 115 founding members across multiple publications are reaping the benefits of early support. I am immensely grateful for these early adopters, and I will reward them in multiple ways.

My goal is to grow this number to 1,000 in the next 12 months, and my aspiration is to have one million founding members in the next 3 to 5 years, expanding our Substack Mastery community to empower freelancers and content entrepreneurs. I also support freelance writers and content entrepreneurs with **free and paid subscriptions on Patreon.**[3]

I believe my modest contributions, with the support of my philanthropic sponsors to this community, will create a ripple effect, helping new freelancers and entrepreneurs thrive.

I am fully committed to their success by offering my support as a thought leader and community builder, using my skills and innovative techniques to help them grow, enjoy their lives, and help improve their readers' lives.

Conclusions and Key Takeaways

FREELANCERS AND CONTENT entrepreneurs depend on income to survive and thrive, but true success is about more than just money — it is about the lasting satisfaction of serving and empowering others.

---

3.   https://digitalmehmet.com/freelance-startup-coaching/

By addressing your readers' needs, solving their challenges, and guiding them toward a better life, you increase your revenue and find deeper meaning and joy in your work.

The discount strategies I introduced in this chapter are not just about boosting sales—they are about building long-term relationships.

By offering value, exclusivity, and personalized offers, you can transform free subscribers into loyal, paying members who become your strongest supporters for a lifetime.

Whether you use special offers or mega discounts (occasionally to celebrate unique wins like mine), these tactics allow you to create a sense of belonging and commitment with your readers, encouraging them to stay engaged and invested in your content.

Take action today — experiment with a small discount or launch a founding membership tier that resonates with your audience's values and needs.

As you do, you will grow your paid subscribers and cultivate a community that supports your vision. The potential is limitless, and it starts with one bold step today.

Chapter 13: 30 Essential Principles for 3 Levels of Freelance iWriters Beyond Substack Offering a Proven Quality Enhancement Checklist

This chapter is different in format and shorter. Although comprehensive, I decided to condense this chapter into an easy-to-follow checklist to help you quickly grasp the essential principles of freelancing beyond Substack. I designed the summary format to provide clarity without overwhelming you with details, allowing you to focus on what's truly important at each stage of your writing and freelancing journey.

As I have already covered most of these topics in the previous **12 chapters,**[1] and the next few chapters dive into advanced strategies, this post serves as a **go-to resource** for organizing and customizing your approach. Whether you are just starting or already scaling, the checklist format offers flexibility to your learning. You can personalize it to meet your unique goals and needs.

I have been using checklists for over 50 years as a lifelong learner in my professional and personal life. They have become indispensable tools for me, especially in my creative and inventive work. Whether I am managing a project, creating a new patent, writing a book, or simply organizing my thoughts, a checklist keeps things clear and actionable.

In fact, as part of my editorial role on this platform, running multiple large publications contributed by thousands of writers, **I introduced multiple quality improvement checklists**[2] to help guide beginner submissions. I saw

---

1.   https://medium.com/illumination/substack-mastery-book-chapter-12-86b59a784fd4

a noticeable improvement in the quality and clarity of the work that came through, delighting readers.

Upon request, I recently created one for aspiring book authors.

<u>**A Comprehensive Quality Control Checklist for Aspiring Book Authors**</u>[3]

<u>I offer a helpful tool to improve the quality of your manuscripts and guide you in finishing your project on time...</u>[4]

Checklists work because they cut through the noise — unlike long, dense submission guidelines that overwhelm people with too much information, they break everything down into manageable steps.

This simple, structured format lets you easily pinpoint where you can improve and grow. It is like having a roadmap that not only helps you stay on track but ensures you are not just ticking off tasks. You are strategically setting yourself up for long-term success.

Why This Checklist Is Essential for Your Freelance Journey

AS A NEW FREELANCER navigating the evolving world of content creation, especially beyond platforms like Substack, achieving success requires more than just passion and creativity.

It demands a methodical (**structured**) **approach** that balances creativity with strategy. That's where this unique checklist reflecting my years of experience comes in. I designed it to guide you through the key principles that successful creators follow to grow, sustain, and scale their platforms as freelancers (solopreneurs) or entrepreneurs.

Whether you are just starting or are well-established, the **30 Principles for Freelancers Beyond Substack** offer a step-by-step roadmap for continuous growth. Here are the three reasons this checklist can be a game-changer for beginners and even other levels who struggle with growth.

---

2. https://medium.com/illumination/improve-the-quality-of-your-stories-blog-posts-or-substack-newsletters-using-editorial-checklists-1e0b4b9cc03e

3. https://medium.com/illumination/a-comprehensive-quality-control-checklist-for-aspiring-book-authors-7564caea5929

4. https://medium.com/illumination/a-comprehensive-quality-control-checklist-for-aspiring-book-authors-7564caea5929

1 — Clarity and Focus: As a beginner, it is easy to feel overwhelmed by all the advice out there. This checklist helps you focus on the most essential steps first, ensuring you build a strong foundation without wasting time.

2 — Momentum and Growth: For intermediate creators, it provides practical strategies to **refine your voice, diversify content, and analyze performance**, helping you stay relevant and continuously improve.

3 — Sustained Success: As an advanced writer, this checklist will assist you in turning your platform into a **scalable business**, with insights on **branding, community building, and advanced monetization**. It equips you with strategies for long-term sustainability, ensuring you don't rely solely on one income stream.

Using this checklist not only helps you stay organized and clear about your goals but also ensures that you evolve as a freelancer in a way that is **strategic, intentional, and scalable**. By breaking down the journey into actionable steps, this resource can turn uncertainty into confidence, and good intentions into real results.

The final version of this book will elaborate on each item on the checklist, offering a more detailed guide for those who want to expand their understanding. For now, I have streamlined the content to avoid overwhelming you with too much information at once.

◈ 30 Principles for 3 Levels of Freelancers Beyond Substack

THIS CHAPTER CONDENSES critical takeaways from previous chapters and introduces advanced concepts that will be covered later.

You may use this as a **customizable checklist** to guide your growth, whether you are a beginner, intermediate, or advanced freelancer.

I am confident about this condensed checklist as I started as a beginner decades ago and now serve as an advanced writer on multiple platforms with over a billion content views and thousands of subscribers.

◈ For Beginners: Laying a Strong Foundation

☑ **Start with Passion**: Write about what excites you — your passion will drive your work.

☑ **Set Clear Goals**: Know what you want to achieve while growing your audience and refining your skills.

☑ **Define Your Niche**: Focus on a topic you know and are deeply connected to.

☑ **Know Your Audience**: Understand your readers' needs and tailor your content accordingly.

☑ **Be Authentic**: Authenticity builds trust. Let your unique voice shine in everything you create.

☑ **Be Consistent**: Develop a posting schedule and stick to it — consistency builds credibility.

☑ **Experiment Early**: Try different formats and topics to discover what resonates with your audience.

☑ **Focus More on Quality Than Quantity**: Prioritize clarity, relevance, and engagement in your writing.

☑ **Engage with Readers**: Respond to comments and start building your community.

☑ **Learn from Others**: Follow successful Substack writers and study their strategies.

◈ For Intermediate Writers: Building Momentum

☑ **Diversify Content Formats**: Use newsletters, stories, interviews, reviews, essays, podcasts, or videos to diversify your content offerings.

☑ **Create a Content Calendar**: Plan content in advance to maintain organization and consistency.

☑ **Refine Your Voice**: Continue to develop your writing style as you grow.

☑ **Expand Your Topics**: Gradually introduce new topics to keep your content fresh and exciting.

☑ **Engage More Deeply**: Add interactive elements like polls or Q&A sessions to enhance engagement.

☑ **Network with Other Writers**: Collaborate with peers through guest posts or partnerships to expand your audience.

☑ **Monetize Thoughtfully**: Start with small monetization steps like paid subscriptions or one-time contributions.

☑ **Use Reader Feedback**: Regularly ask for and integrate reader feedback to improve your work.

☑ **Stay Informed**: Stay updated on industry trends to keep your content relevant and forward-thinking.

☑ **Analyze Performance**: Use analytics to learn what's working and where you can improve.

◈ For Advanced Writers: Scaling & Sustaining Success

☑ **Build a Brand Owning Your Site**: Treat your platform as a personal brand. Maintain consistency in your tone, visuals, and messaging.

☑ **Plan for Longevity**: Think long-term. How will your platform evolve over the next few years?

☑ **Optimize for Growth**: Implement referral programs, partnerships, or other scaling strategies.

☑ **Explore Advanced Monetization**: Look into premium content, online courses, affiliate marketing, or sponsored posts as ways to increase revenue.

☑ **Diversify Revenue Streams**: Don't depend on one source of income; explore ads, merchandise, and multiple subscription models.

☑ **Invest in Professional Tools**: Upgrade to advanced tools for analytics, email marketing, and content creation to enhance efficiency.

☑ **Automate Where Possible**: Use automation tools to manage routine tasks like scheduling, email replies, and social media posts.

☑ **Offer Personalized Content**: Segment your audience and provide tailored content for more personalized interactions.

☑ **Host Local Events or Global Webinars**: Engage your audience with live events to deepen relationships and offer value.

☑ **Strengthen Community Ties**: Promote a strong sense of community by offering regular engagement, exclusive content, and perks.

Conclusions and Key Takeaways

BY FOLLOWING THIS PROVEN checklist and tailoring it to your needs, you will have a clear path to evolve from a beginner to an advanced freelancer, honing in on the critical elements that drive lasting success. You will keep the momentum.

I designed it to be adaptable to your specific goals and flexible enough to evolve as you grow in your freelance journey. Remember, this checklist is not tied to any particular platform — whether it is Substack or another- and these principles hold true across the board. Platforms may come and go, but the wisdom within these steps is timeless.

Feel free to share this checklist so more people can benefit from it. If you decide to publish it in your blogs, articles, or newsletters, please credit the **original source**[5], as I may update this content in the future based on feedback and new insights from discerning readers.

Thank you for reading my perspectives. I wish you a healthy and happy life.

Invitation to Be a Guest Blogger

I RECENTLY OPENED MY website to welcome all writers as guest bloggers, offering a platform to boost visibility for your profiles, Medium stories, and Substack newsletters.

I've outlined the compelling reasons to join our community blog in detail, making it an ideal space for authentic and ethical writers who want to share their work freely.

<u>**Here's Why I Opened My Website to Freelance Writers as Guest Bloggers from Multiple Platforms**</u>[6]

<u>I explain why and how writers can benefit from this free blogging opportunity, empowered by a non-commercial writing...</u>[7]

Here, **no legal content is censored!** I strongly value **diversity, inclusion, and equality** in distributing content. If you want a supportive environment to

---

5.   https://digitalmehmet.com/2024/09/18/substack-mastery-book-chapter-13/

6.   https://medium.com/illumination/heres-why-i-opened-my-website-to-freelance-writers-as-guest-bloggers-on-multiple-platforms-39c03d8c8409

7.   https://medium.com/illumination/heres-why-i-opened-my-website-to-freelance-writers-as-guest-bloggers-on-multiple-platforms-39c03d8c8409

amplify your voice, I have created **this accessible and supportive place**[8] for you.

---

8. https://digitalmehmet.com/blog-posts/

Chapter 14: How to Add Interactive Educational Programs Using One of the 6 Globally Recognized Tools to Inform, Educate, Inspire, and Retain Your Subscribers

I designed this chapter specifically for those looking to expand their writing and coaching businesses by adding educational programs or digital products. While creating these programs can be challenging, especially for those without technical expertise, numerous well-established service providers can handle the technical aspects and simplify the process.

As a content development and marketing strategist, I have evaluated many tools and products for my clients in the content entrepreneurship space. In this chapter, I will present eight popular tools my clients, collaborators, students, and proteges use successfully for their growth.

As my comprehensive assessments for paid clients span over 300 pages of information report and it is impossible to cover so many details in a single chapter of this book, I will provide a concise overview of these tools, including their focus, benefits, and potential drawbacks.

I will also show indicative cost information to help you make informed decisions based on your budget. While I have hands-on experience with some of these tools, I will also include feedback from others to provide a balanced perspective. I aim to inform and encourage you to research tools to help you grow your freelance writing business.

Introduction to 6 Globally Recognized Tools for

Course Development and Marketing

I HAVE LISTED THEM based on their popularity and market shares.

1 — Udemy

UDEMY WENT PUBLIC IN 2021 with a market value of about $3.25 billion. It is a popular online course marketplace with a large, built-in audience, making it easy for instructors to reach learners without the need for marketing or website setup.

One of Udemy's main advantages is its massive audience, which helps instructors attract students more easily. It's also simple to get started since Udemy handles most of the technical work.

However, a key drawback is that instructors have limited control over pricing, branding, and how much money they earn. Udemy takes a significant portion of the revenue unless instructors drive their traffic.

It's free to join, but Udemy keeps 50% of sales through its platform, while instructors keep 97% through their referral links.

Udemy's recent introduction of the 'Udemy Business' model offers instructors more customization and control, making it suitable for those who need greater flexibility. I will write a detailed article about this new business model soon.

2 — Kajabi

AFTER ITS FIRST FUNDING round in 2021, Kajabi was valued at around $550 million. It is an all-in-one platform for creating, selling, and managing digital products and online businesses.

Kajabi offers comprehensive tools for course creation, marketing, sales funnels, and website building. It might be ideal for creators who want full control over every aspect of their business, from branding to pricing.

The platform's main advantage is its robust features, which allow creators to manage everything in one place. However, Kajabi's higher price point may be a drawback for beginners or smaller creators who don't need all its advanced features. The cost starts at $149 per month for the Basic plan, $199 per month for the Growth plan, and $399 per month for the pro plan.

From my observations, Kajabi's built-in email marketing features and advanced automation capabilities make it an ideal choice for creators who want to streamline their marketing and sales processes

3 — Teachable

IN 2020, TEACHABLE was acquired by Hotmart Group for $250 million. Teachable is an online course platform designed to make course creation, sales, and management easy for instructors.

Teachable's main advantages include intuitive course creation tools, flexible course pricing options, and global VAT handling, making it convenient for instructors selling courses worldwide. Teachable also offers multiple pricing plans to fit different needs.

However, compared to more comprehensive platforms like Kajabi, Teachable has limited website customization and fewer marketing tools. Its free plan has a $1 + 10% fee per sale, while paid plans start at $39 per month and have lower transaction fees on higher-tier plans.

4 — Thinkific

I NOTICED THAT THINKIFIC'S market capitalization was around $180 million. Thinkific is a course creation platform designed for educators and entrepreneurs who want more customization and control over their online courses.

Thinkific offers customization options, flexible course delivery formats, and the ability to integrate with third-party tools, giving creators much flexibility. However, one drawback is that Thinkific lacks built-in email marketing and advanced sales funnels so that users may need external tools for complete marketing automation.

Thinkific offers a free plan, while paid plans start at $49 per month for the Basic plan, $99 per month for the Pro plan, and $499 for the Premier plan.

While Thinkific doesn't have built-in email marketing or advanced sales funnels, it integrates seamlessly with popular third-party tools like Mailchimp and Zapier, providing flexibility for creators who prefer external solutions.

5 — Podia

PODIA IS PRIVATELY held and has a smaller market share compared to Kajabi. Podia is a simple platform for selling courses, memberships, and digital products, making it especially user-friendly for beginners.

Podia's key advantages include ease of use, no transaction fees, and lower pricing compared to platforms like Kajabi and Thinkific.

However, Podia offers fewer marketing and automation tools and lacks advanced customization options, which may be a limitation for creators seeking more robust features. Pricing starts at $39 per month for the Mover plan, $89 per month for the Shaker plan, and $199 for the Earthquaker plan.

6 — WordPress with Plugins (LearnDash, WooCommerce)

WHILE WORDPRESS IS an open-source project, its parent company, Automattic, was valued at over $7 billion as of 2023. With plugins like LearnDash and WooCommerce which I covered **on my website**[1], WordPress offers a highly customizable setup for creators who want full control over their website, content, and courses.

The main advantage is that it provides complete control over branding, design, and functionality while integrating seamlessly with many third-party tools and plugins, such as LearnDash for course creation and WooCommerce for eCommerce.

However, it requires technical knowledge for setup and ongoing maintenance, including hosting, updates, and security. Costs vary depending on hosting, which ranges from $5 to $25 per month, and plugin expenses, with LearnDash starting at $199 per year, while WooCommerce is free but may require paid add-ons.

---

1. **https://digitalmehmet.com/selected-and-recommended-products/**

As a long-term user, I know that WordPress offers unparalleled customization and control, making it a popular choice for creators who want to build a unique and personalized learning experience.

Landing Pages and Funnel-Building for Marketing and Sales of Educational Products

ADVANCED FREELANCE writers and content entrepreneurs use automation tools to optimize their marketing sales processes for their educational tools. If you are not using the previously mentioned course creation platforms, you might need tools like ClickFunnels or Kartra, which I will introduce in this section.

These platforms are famous for building landing pages and sales funnels used by millions of content developers and marketers. I will briefly introduce both to help you find the best fit for your needs. I also mention the names of their competitors in the next section to make your research easier.

For those unfamiliar, **"Landing Pages and Funnel-Building"** refer to the creation of specialized web pages and sales processes designed to capture leads, drive conversions, and guide potential customers through a structured buying journey.

Freelancers and content entrepreneurs can use landing pages to promote offers, collect email addresses, and engage visitors. They also use marketing and sales funnels to create strategic sequences of pages and actions that nurture leads and convert them into paying customers.

Effective marketing and sales funnel building involves designing processes to optimize the user experience and maximize conversions, using tools that streamline and automate these tasks.

1 — ClickFunnels

CLICKFUNNELS (AS I introduced **on my website**[2]) is a funnel-building platform designed to create high-converting sales and landing pages.

---

2. https://digitalmehmet.com/selected-and-recommended-products/

ClickFunnels is an excellent choice for marketers selling services and digital/physical products. It offers helpful tools for marketing/sales funnels and conversions.

However, ClickFunnels has limited course hosting and content creation capabilities, so users might need another platform to manage their courses, as I introduced in the previous section

The basic plan costs $147 per month, the pro plan costs $297 per month, and the Funnel Hacker plan costs $497. ClickFunnels is valued at over $360 million.

2 — Kartra

KARTRA IS AN ALL-IN-one platform for managing online businesses. It offers tools for marketing and sales funnels, memberships, and email marketing.

Kartra is a comprehensive solution with powerful affiliate marketing management and automation features. However, from my clients' experiences, it seems to have a steeper learning curve than other platforms and fewer course creation resources than Teachable or Thinkific.

Pricing starts at $99 per month for the Starter plan and goes up to $499 for the Platinum plan. Kartra is privately held and has a smaller market share than Kajabi and ClickFunnels.

Competitors of ClickFunnels or Kartra

MANY OTHER OPTIONS are available, but these are among the most popular. I have had the opportunity to evaluate and learn about them through insights from users who have implemented them. I will give you a few examples for your assessment.

While **ClickFunnels**[3], Leadpages, and Unbounce specialize in landing page creation and A/B testing (comparing 2 versions of a webpage), other platforms offer comprehensive features for online courses, including sales funnels, email marketing, and automation.

Builderall provides an all-in-one solution for these needs. GetResponse integrates funnel-building, email marketing, and landing pages, with additional

---

3.   https://digitalmehmet.com/selected-and-recommended-products/

features like built-in webinars tailored for online courses. Instapage excels in advanced landing page optimization and personalization, which can be particularly valuable for promoting courses.

5 Key Considerations When Choosing a Platform

SELECTING THE RIGHT platform depends on various factors unique to your needs, goals, and aspirations. Based on my experience, I will provide some key considerations and tips to guide your decision-making process.

1 — Your Goals and Needs

START BY IDENTIFYING where you are in your freelancing journey. Are you a beginner just starting out or an experienced creator looking to scale? For beginners, a simple, user-friendly platform like Podia or Teachable may be ideal due to their ease of use and lower learning curve.

On the other hand, experienced creators who need more advanced features and customization may prefer platforms like Kajabi or WordPress with plugins, as these offer greater control over branding, pricing, and functionality.

Example: A new course creator might choose Teachable because it is easy to set up and manage, while an established entrepreneur might opt for Kajabi for its robust sales funnels and marketing tools.

2 — Current Budget and Long-Term Financial Consideration

YOUR BUDGET AND FINANCIAL plans can play a crucial role in your decision. While a platform like Udemy allows you to join for free, they take a large portion of your earnings.

Other platforms, like Thinkific and Kajabi, have monthly fees but offer more control over your business. It is essential to weigh the cost against the value of the features you'll use.

Example: If you are starting with a smaller budget, Thinkific's $49/month Basic plan could be a good entry point. However, if you want a comprehensive suite of tools, Kajabi's $149/month plan may offer better value in the long run.

3 — Functions and Features

YOU NEED TO EVALUATE each platform's feature set in relation to your specific needs. Do you need strong course creation tools, or are you looking for additional features like membership sites, email marketing, or affiliate management?

Platforms like Kajabi and Kartra offer all-in-one solutions with a wide range of features, whereas platforms like Teachable focus more on course creation and management.

Example: If you want to run membership programs or manage email marketing from one platform, Kartra might be a better fit than Teachable, which focuses primarily on courses.

4 — Customization

YOU NEED TO DETERMINE how much control you want over your website's design and functionality. A popular platform like WordPress with plugins (LearnDash, WooCommerce) offers full control over every aspect of your site, but they require technical knowledge.

Conversely, platforms like Podia and Teachable offer pre-designed templates, which are easier to set up but less customizable.

Example: If you have web development skills and want a fully customized site, WordPress might be a good choice. If you prefer a quick, ready-to-use solution, Podia's simpler setup may work better.

5 — Support and Resources

YOU ALSO NEED TO CONSIDER the level of customer support and educational resources available from each platform. Some platforms offer extensive knowledge bases, live chat, or community support, which can be invaluable, especially if you're new to the process.

Kajabi, for instance, is known for its excellent customer support and training resources, while WordPress requires more self-management or third-party assistance unless you have a business or premium account.

So, if customer support is a priority for you, Kajabi's responsive support team may be more helpful than WordPress, where you will need to rely on forums or hire outside help for technical issues.

Conclusions and Key Takeaways

SELECTING THE RIGHT online course platform requires careful consideration of your goals, needs, budget, features, customization requirements, support, and scalability. By clearly assessing these factors, you can choose a platform that aligns with your needs, budget, and long-term business goals.

By evaluating these factors, experimenting, and learning from others' experiences, you can choose a platform that aligns with your long-term business objectives and provides the necessary tools and resources to succeed in the online education market.

Additionally, exploring the community and network associated with each platform can provide valuable insights and support. By making an informed decision, you can create a thriving online course business and reach a broader audience of learners.

As a solopreneur or entrepreneur, you must align your platform choice with your long-term strategy and growth plans. Ensure that the platform you select can adapt to your evolving needs and scale alongside your business expansion.

It would help to consider how well it supports your current objectives and whether it can accommodate future growth, from increased traffic and sales to advanced features and customization. This strategic alignment will help you avoid potential disruptions and ensure a seamless growth trajectory.

Even if you don't use educational programs in your service offering, as freelance writers and content entrepreneurs, you must use landing pages on your platforms to promote offers, collect email addresses, and engage visitors. You can also use marketing and sales funnels to create strategic sequences of pages and actions that nurture leads and convert them into paying customers.

Feel free to share this chapter so more people can benefit from it. If you decide to publish it in your blogs, articles, or newsletters, please credit the

original source[4], as I may update this content in the future based on feedback and new insights from discerning readers.

---

4.   https://digitalmehmet.com/2024/09/18/educational-tools-for-freelancers/

Chapter 15: Why and How to Integrate Substack with Patreon for Compelling Reasons

I crafted this chapter with advanced writers in mind, but I also offer valuable insights for newcomers too. Whether you use Substack and Patreon separately or together, integrating them — like I do and many other established creators — can yield powerful results.

In this chapter, I shall share my thoughts, experiences, and observations on Patreon and encourage freelance writers and content entrepreneurs to consider pairing it with Substack. Both platforms are excellent, each offering unique ways to support creators.

While I am unsure how these companies see each other, I view them not as competitors but as complementary services that can work together to enhance your creative reach. As a personal principle, I never see others as competitors but as collaborators — and this mindset has worked wonders for me.

Why Patreon Is Important for Substack Writers, Freelancers, and Content Entrepreneurs from 8 Different Aspects

PATREON IS A UNIQUE platform for creators, freelance writers, and content entrepreneurs because it offers a reliable way to diversify income, connect with audiences, and scale creative businesses. In this section, I will provide a high-level perspective on the benefits of Patreon based on my experience and observations of other creators.

1 — Creative Freedom

ON PATREON, CREATORS are in control of their content and how they monetize it. Unlike traditional freelance jobs or corporate-sponsored gigs, creators are not bound by strict guidelines, allowing them to experiment and pursue projects that align with their creative vision. A Substack writer, for example, might use Patreon to fund a long-form investigative series they couldn't pitch to mainstream publications.

2 — Direct Audience Support

PATREON ALLOWS CONTENT creators to build a community of loyal supporters who value their work. By engaging directly with their audience, creators can offer exclusive perks such as early access, bonus content, or personalized shoutouts that make patrons feel appreciated. This direct support model can empower creators to focus on their passion without relying on third-party platforms or advertisers. For instance, a writer can create tiers of support where patrons who pay $10 a month can access bonus essays, stories, or behind-the-scenes insights into their products.

3 — Enhanced Community Building

PATREON HELPS CULTIVATE a deeper connection between creators and their audience by offering private forums, Questions and Answers (Q&A) sessions and other interactive opportunities. This sense of community can turn casual readers or followers into dedicated fans, creating a core group of emotionally invested supporters in the creator's success. Content entrepreneurs use Patreon to nurture an intimate space for their significant supporters. For example, musicians might host Patreon-exclusive live streams, or writers might hold Q&A sessions about their book launches.

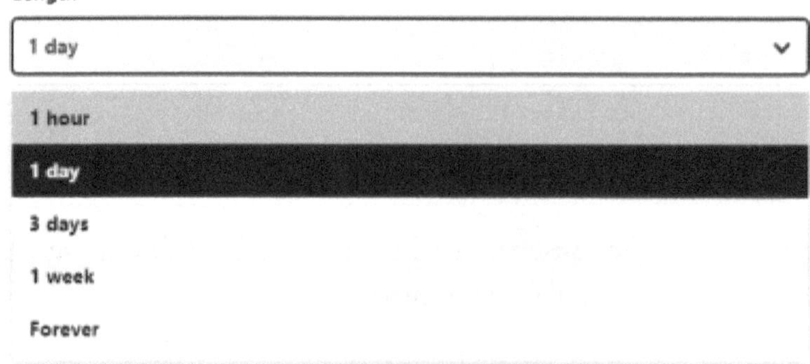

YOU CAN ADD UP TO FIVE options.

The length has the following options:

You can choose all subscribers or only paid ones.

4 — Financial Support from Patrons

FREELANCERS AND CONTENT creators face inconsistent pay. With Patreon, creators can receive recurring monthly payments from subscribers (patrons) who support their work. This steady income stream can offer financial stability crucial for freelancers, especially when other revenue streams like ads, sponsorships, or commissions fluctuate. For example, a Substack writer who offers exclusive content on Patreon might get a reliable $5 per patron each month, which can help cover expenses.

5 — Diversification of Revenue Streams

FOR FREELANCERS AND entrepreneurs who already earn money from other platforms like Substack or YouTube, Patreon provides an additional revenue stream. This diversification is critical to long-term financial success, as relying solely on one platform can be risky. For instance, a freelance journalist might use Substack for email subscriptions but offer Patreon supporters early drafts, unpublished stories, or writing workshops to maximize earnings.

6 — Tailored Membership Options

PATREON'S TIERED MEMBERSHIP model allows creators to design different levels of support, each offering unique perks. This allows them to cater to various types of fans. For example, a $1 tier might offer general support, while a $50 tier could include personalized feedback or direct communication. This flexible model makes it easy for creators to grow their income as their audience expands, offering something valuable for both casual supporters and die-hard fans.

7 — Monetizing Niche Content

FINDING ADVERTISERS or sponsorships can be challenging for creators in smaller or niche industries. Patreon allows even small-scale creators to make money by connecting with audiences that appreciate their specialized work.

Whether it's a podcast about obscure history, a newsletter on sustainable farming, or personal essays on mental health, Patreon allows creators to get paid for content that might not have mainstream appeal but resonates deeply with their audience.

8 — Global Reach

WITH PATREON, CREATORS can reach patrons around the world, allowing them to monetize their content globally. It opens up opportunities for creators in smaller markets to gain international supporters. For example, an independent artist from a small town can still attract patrons from big cities globally who love their unique style and are willing to support their work.

Summary of Key Benefits of Integrating Patreon with Substack

BY LEVERAGING THE POWER of Patreon and Substack, freelance writers, book authors, and other content creators like bloggers or copywriters can build a sustainable and scalable income model, balancing free public content with exclusive paid experiences. Here are the key points:

Combining Substack's subscription-based newsletters with Patreon's tiered membership system offers multiple revenue sources. Patreon offers interactive features to engage with supporters on a more personal level.

You can reserve your best content for paying patrons on Patreon while using Substack as a way to reach a broader audience. Patreon's recurring memberships allow for predictable, passive income, while Substack continues to attract new readers.

What Distinguishes Patreon from Substack

WHILE BOTH PATREON and Substack provide monetization opportunities for creators, they differ significantly in their approach, features, and audience engagement methods. In this section, I will provide a high-level comparative perspective on what distinguishes Patreon from Substack and how Patreon can fill gaps for creators, freelance writers, and content entrepreneurs.

1 — Subscription vs. Patronage

SUBSTACK: Substack's model is subscription-based, where users pay a flat fee to receive content. It is great for writers who want to build a paid newsletter and create regular income from their subscribers.

Patreon: Patreon operates on a patronage model, where supporters contribute to creators on an ongoing basis for access to special perks. Patrons feel like they support the creator personally rather than paying strictly for content, which encourages more emotional investment in the creator's success.

Gap Filled by Patreon: While Substack subscribers are paying for access to a product (your newsletter), Patreon allows your audience to feel like they are supporting you as a creator. This creates a stronger, more personal bond between the creator and the audience. A Substack writer could use Patreon to attract fans who want to support their overall creative work, not just the newsletter.

2 — Monetization Models

SUBSTACK: Substack primarily focuses on free or paid email newsletters. Writers can charge subscribers for exclusive content, with Substack taking a 10% cut of revenue. Monetization is straightforward, based mostly on the subscription model for written content.

Patreon: Patreon offers a more flexible tiered membership system, where creators can offer different levels of content and benefits based on how much a patron contributes. This allows creators to set multiple price points for various perks, such as early access to content, personalized shoutouts, or behind-the-scenes updates. Patreon also supports more than just written content, allowing creators to offer exclusive videos, podcasts, artwork, digital books, and other media forms.

Gap Filled by Patreon: Substack is limited to two subscription prices (basic membership and founding tier), which may not cater to different levels of fan engagement. Patreon's multiple-tiered system allows freelance writers to create different levels of perks and charge accordingly, increasing their potential earnings. For example, a writer might offer early drafts of their work or personalized feedback on patrons' writing at a higher tier, something they couldn't do easily on Substack.

3 — Content Types and Flexibility

SUBSTACK: Substack is optimized for written content, especially email newsletters. It is primarily text-driven, though it has recently supported some audio and podcast integrations, which is a good thing.

Patreon: Patreon supports a broader content type, such as videos, podcasts, artwork, photography, digital books, and live streams. This flexibility allows creators to diversify their offerings and build multimedia content that can complement their written work.

Gap Filled by Patreon: As a freelance writer, you may feel limited by the text-centric nature of the Substack platform. Patreon allows you to supplement your newsletters with additional media, like hosting live discussions, offering video breakdowns of your essays, or sharing exclusive podcasts that dive deeper into your writing topics. This multimedia approach engages your audience in new ways, deepening your connection with them.

4 — Enhanced Community Engagement and Interaction

SUBSTACK: Substack offers limited tools for audience engagement, mainly through comments and email interactions. Writers can engage with their readers via replies to newsletters or comments on posts and Notes, but the engagement is typically one-dimensional and not real-time.

Patreon: Patreon excels at facilitating community interaction. It offers a space for creators to engage more **intimately** with their audience through private forums, direct messaging, and live Q&A sessions or streams. Patreon creators can also reward their most loyal supporters with exclusive content, polls, and patron-only updates.

Gap Filled by Patreon: If you are a Substack writer looking to build a more interactive community, Patreon might fill this gap by offering enhanced engagement tools. For instance, you can set up private discussion forums for your patrons, host live chats, or share personal updates that help cultivate a deeper connection with your audience.

5 — Creator-Controlled Perks

SUBSTACK: The perks on Substack are tied to the subscription model, so your main value proposition is the content you send via email newsletters. Any additional perks like special shoutouts or private meetups would have to be manually managed by the creator outside of Substack's platform.

Patreon: Patreon allows for more structured and diverse perks tied to membership tiers. You can offer various rewards depending on the level of support, such as exclusive content, personalized advice, physical merchandise, or early access to new projects. These perks are integrated into Patreon's system, making it easier to manage.

Gap Filled by Patreon: For Substack writers looking to offer more personalized perks, Patreon provides a built-in system for offering tiered benefits without the manual tracking that would be required on Substack. For example, you could offer personal coaching sessions, handwritten letters, or exclusive merchandise at higher tiers to create a unique and more immersive experience for your most engaged readers.

6 — Exclusive Community Features

SUBSTACK: Substack offers fewer gated community features than paid newsletters and private posts.

Patreon: Patreon lets creators offer exclusive content and experiences to their patrons. Whether it is a live hangout, a behind-the-scenes look at the writing process, or a private discussion group, Patreon builds exclusivity into its structure.

Gap Filled by Patreon: Writers on Substack could use Patreon to build a VIP community for their most loyal fans. You might offer early drafts of upcoming newsletters or books, invite patrons to help shape future content, or provide private webinars. This creates an "inner circle" feel that Substack alone cannot provide.

7 — Revenue Diversification

SUBSTACK: Substack writers can earn through subscriptions, and some writers may choose to accept tips or donations, though these features are not central to the platform.

Patreon: Patreon allows creators to diversify their income through monthly contributions, higher-tiered memberships, special patron-only events, or even limited-time offers (like offering a personalized writing critique for patrons at a higher level).

Gap Filled by Patreon: Patreon helps writers on Substack diversify their revenue beyond the traditional subscription model. You could, for example, offer writing workshops or behind-the-scenes essays to patrons who support you at higher tiers or run short-term campaigns where higher-paying patrons receive exclusive benefits, such as book pre-orders or signed copies of your work.

7 — Merchandising and Special Campaigns

SUBSTACK: Substack is currently limited to newsletters and digital content, with no native features for merchandising or running special campaigns.

Patreon: Patreon allows creators to offer merchandise, run special campaigns (e.g., a month-long initiative for new patrons), and offer physical products like books, T-shirts, mugs, cards, or personalized items as perks for higher-paying patrons.

Gap Filled by Patreon: For Substack writers with a broader vision for their content brand, Patreon can offer merchandising and special campaign opportunities to engage patrons more deeply. For instance, you could run a campaign where patrons at a certain tier receive a signed copy of your latest book or a custom-designed piece of merchandise tied to your content.

A Sample Case Study to Integrate Substack with Patreon

IN THE LAST FEW MONTHS, one of my popular Substack newsletters, **Content Strategy, Development, & Marketing Insights**[1], which I have been giving as a free service for over five years, gained momentum when I decided to reduce my time on Medium and increase on Substack, which also coincided with writing this book.

Some of my mentors like **Tim Denning** [2]advised me to monetize my content while still giving free content on Substack will have no motivation to promote my newsletters. He was absolutely right because as soon as I turned on monetization, my newsletters spiked and grew by at least 600% within the last few months. I have never witnessed such a growth on Substack.

Gaining many paid members and even some founding members inspired me. I started interacting with them more often via emails and Substack Notes. However, some members found the interactions difficult and insufficient. They wanted to have a closer and more intimate environment to communicate and gain access to me more easily.

As I have been using Patreon for this purpose with my clients for special projects like invention workshops, design thinking workshops, co-authoring papers, or collaborative book projects, I decided to open a new Patreon account to support freelance writers. I called it **Freelance Startup Support and Coaching**[3].

My Patreon address is: https://www.patreon.com/drmehmetyildiz

I designed the space in 4 tiers.

The first tier is for free members to explore and understand the nature of work in this space. I offer several articles and summaries of books for free to these members. It shows at the bottom of my service membership page[4] like the following screen capture.

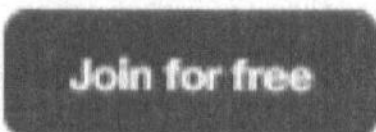

source[5]

---

1. https://drmehmetyildiz.substack.com/

2. https://medium.com/illumination/why-did-i-interview-my-aussie-friend-tim-denning-again-on-medium-substack-f44257d456ef

3. https://www.patreon.com/drmehmetyildiz/membership

4. https://www.patreon.com/drmehmetyildiz/membership

THE SECOND TIER IS called Writing & Content Development Support, with a minimum allowable cost of $3 USD. I wanted to make it cheaper, but like Substack, Patreon does not allow us to do so. I provide writing tips for creating articles, blogs, papers, and non-fiction books. I continue adding content relating to writing, editing, blogging, and publishing for freelance writers.

The third tier is called **Guidance, Help & Promotion.** In addition to writing and content development, I provide promotion, blogging, Substack, and social media support to help promote your content (articles, papers, podcasts, books). I also answer queries via email, Slack, or Substack Notes for this tier. I offer this service for $10 USD as it requires additional time and effort.

The fourth tier is called **Professional Coaching & Partnership**. This is my premium service covering many professional support services, including writing/editing tips, freelancing support, blogging, guest blogging, Substack Mastery membership, social media support, technology advice, small business development ideas, Startup coaching, publishing guidance, and affiliate marketing support for freelance writers and content entrepreneurs. I offer this service for $30 USD as it requires more time and effort.

In addition, I experimented with offering one book as a digital product at half the price of its market value in other bookshops, and some members loved buying it for a lower price. I experimented with a few high-impact articles for one-time buyers with a minimum price of $3 and will add more as soon as there is a demand for them.

Although we can market our books or paid articles on Substack, we can't directly sell them. However, we can do it on Patreon; therefore, integrating two platforms is an excellent choice.

How does Patreon compare to Substack in Charging Creators?

THIS IS THE MOST FREQUENTLY asked question by my clients, colleagues, friends, students, and proteges; therefore, I decided to create a section for it.

---

5. https://www.patreon.com/drmehmetyildiz/membership

As I mentioned in previous chapters, Substack charges a **flat 10% fee** on earnings. However, Patreon offers **a tiered system** with more flexibility depending on the services a creator wants to access.

The good news for global creators is that Patreon uses PayPal, which is more accepted globally and much easier than Stripe.

I want to point out that with Patreon, additional fees for payment processing and payouts might lead to a slightly higher total deduction, especially when smaller donations are made. Patreon's fees vary by plan and transaction size, but the structure provides options for creators based on their needs, offering more control over their business model than Substack's flat fee.

Here is a breakdown from my experience:

Patreon uses a tiered fee structure to charge creators, and the amount they take depends on the plan chosen by the creator. Here's how Patreon charges creators:

Patreon platform fee:

Lite plan: 5% of the monthly earnings. **Pro plan**: 8% of the monthly earnings. **Premium plan**: 12% of the monthly earnings (this plan includes additional services like dedicated partner management).

Payment processing fee:

For donations over $3: around **2.9% + $0.30** per transaction. For donations under $3: around **5% + $0.10** per transaction.

Payout fees:

When creators withdraw their earnings, there is an additional fee for transferring funds, which varies based on the payout method (bank transfer, PayPal, etc.).

Conclusions and Key Takeaways

PATREON CAN BE VALUABLE for creators, freelancers, and content entrepreneurs because it enables them to generate consistent income, connect with their audience on a deeper level, and maintain creative freedom. Whether it's a podcaster, artist, or writer, Patreon offers a flexible and reliable platform for turning passion projects into sustainable careers.

Patreon is a membership platform that allows creators, including freelance writers, authors, storytellers, editors, and digital marketers, to receive financial support directly from their audience through subscriptions. Supporters, called "patrons," can choose to pledge a certain amount monthly in exchange for exclusive content, behind-the-scenes access, early releases, or other perks.

For freelance writers and content creators, particularly those using platforms like Substack, Patreon offers a way to diversify income streams by offering additional membership tiers and exclusive benefits beyond what's shared publicly.

Patreon provides insights into your patrons' engagement, including which tiers are most popular and how your audience interacts with your content. This information might help refine your content strategy, complementing Substack's analytics on newsletter performance so you can optimize both platforms for passive income.

When we look at the big picture, success hinges on creating content that resonates deeply with your audience in today's digital landscape. Writers can build meaningful connections beyond metrics by embracing strategic storytelling, consistency, and authentic engagement.

Satisfaction for creators is not about chasing virality but enabling trust and delivering value that stands the test of time. Each piece of content should reflect your unique voice while addressing the needs and curiosity of your readers. As you move forward, focus on being intentional, impactful, and adaptable. This is the path to sustainable growth and lasting influence in an ever-evolving online world.

Platforms like Substack, Patreon, and Medium are valuable tools for diversifying your content and income streams, but they should never be your only foundation. As your audience and influence grow, it is crucial to invest in building your platform — something you fully control.

These tools, while powerful, can change or even disappear, but your own platform ensures lasting security and independence for your creative work. Think of it as safeguarding your future so your voice is always heard, no matter how the landscape evolves.

Chapter 16: How to Use Online Polls on Substack Effectively to Improve Your Content and Grow Your Audience

Introduction

I have been using surveys and polls for many years. Polls are quick and narrow in scope, while surveys are more detailed and aim to collect deeper insights. They have helped me gather information and validate my hypotheses during my postgraduate studies, enabling me to produce more reliable and engaging content in my papers and books.

I have also used polls in client engagements to provide better insights, on social media platforms like LinkedIn to enhance my knowledge, and within my Slack workspace to obtain consent from editors for publishing or curation decisions on high-impact stories within my community.

Polls have been a staple for researchers, marketers, sales professionals, and anyone looking to enhance their data and present more reliable information.

For those unfamiliar, an **online poll** is a digital survey tool used to collect opinions, feedback, or valuable data from participants over the Internet using various sites and tools. These polls typically consist of a question or series of questions with predefined answer choices, allowing users to quickly select their response.

Online polls are used on websites, social media posts, newsletters, and email campaigns to engage audiences, collect real-time data, and analyze trends.

Results are usually displayed instantly, making them an interactive and efficient way to gather insights on various topics.

There are various types of polls, but in this post, I will focus on one specific type used in Substack with limited options. I hope Substack improves this tool to make it more valuable for writers. Online polls can be a helpful tool for freelance writers, offering a means to engage with your audience, gather feedback, and validate content ideas.

Purpose of the Chapter

IN THIS CHAPTER, WE will explore why freelance writers should use polls, the benefits they can derive from them. I will provide examples, and share best practices to inform, educate, and inspire you to use them in your craft.

The Importance of Using Online Polls on Substack

TO GIVE AN EXAMPLE to freelance writers, I created a sample poll on Substack in which you can participate and share your thoughts. The question is, "**As a Freelance Writer, Which Writing Platform(s) Do You Prefer?[1]**"

As a Freelance Writer, Which Writing Platform(s) Do You Prefer?[2]

An online poll to identify the effectiveness of major writing platforms with feedback from participants **drmehmetyildiz.substack.com[3]**

If you don't have time to read this story, you can listen to the audio version of it summarized by **ILLUMINATION-Curators[4]** in a 5-minute interactive podcast using Google's NKLM tool.

Audio Summary of Chapter 17 in Substack Mastery Book by Dr Mehmet Yildiz[5]

How to Use Online Polls on Substack Effectively to Improve Your Content and Grow Your Audience **illuminationcurators.substack.com[6]**

---

1. https://drmehmetyildiz.substack.com/p/as-a-freelance-writer-which-writing

2.   https://drmehmetyildiz.substack.com/p/as-a-freelance-writer-which-writing

3.   https://drmehmetyildiz.substack.com/p/as-a-freelance-writer-which-writing

4.   https://medium.com/u/3ed16e2a5be

5.   https://illuminationcurators.substack.com/p/audio-summary-of-chapter-17-in-substack

6.   https://illuminationcurators.substack.com/p/audio-summary-of-chapter-17-in-substack

8 Reasons Why Freelance Writers Might Use Online Polls

BY USING POLLS, YOU engage your audience and gain valuable insights that can enhance your content strategy, improve retention, and drive growth.

There might be more reasons for your needs and aspirations, but for those who haven't used them, I'd like to summarize the reasons I have been using polls as a researcher for qualitative and quantitative data collection.

1 — **Validate content:** Test new ideas or angles before fully developing them into articles.

2 — **Boost engagement:** Polls encourage interaction, making readers feel involved in the content creation and marketing processes.

3 — **Gather feedback:** Understand your audience's preferences and tailor your content accordingly.

4 — **Build community:** Create a sense of belonging as readers share their opinions and see the responses of others.

5 — **Increase Open Rates:** Using polls in your newsletters can pique curiosity, encouraging more readers to open up and engage with your content.

6 — **Inspire New Content Ideas:** Discover topics your audience is eager to learn about and use them to guide your content calendar.

7 — **Enhance Personalization**: Ask readers about their specific interests or challenges, which allows you to customize content for different segments of your audience.

8 — **Drive Subscription Growth**: Use polls to understand what motivates your readers to subscribe and what additional content they value.

8 — Benefits of Online Polls

FROM MY EXPERIENCE, I'd like to share some benefits I gained using polls on different platforms, which can also provide similar benefits on Substack.

1 — **Data Collection**: Polls provide valuable data that can inform your future content and marketing strategies.

2 — **Increased Retention**: Engaging readers with polls can increase retention rates as they feel their opinions matter.

3 — Enhanced Insights: Analyzing poll results can give you deeper insights into your audience's preferences and pain points.

4 — Content Inspiration: Poll results can spark new ideas for articles, making your writing more relevant and timely.

5 — Create Authenticity: Polls allow you to show your audience that you value their opinions, creating a more authentic connection.

6 — Encourage Social Sharing: Interesting poll results can motivate readers to share their opinions on social media, expanding your reach.

7 — Measure Engagement Trends: Using polls allows you to track engagement over time, identifying what content consistently resonates with your audience.

8 — Create Opportunities for Follow-Up Content: Poll results can highlight topics that warrant deeper exploration, providing clear directions for future articles, stories, or books for creators.

Sample Polls to Inspire Freelance Writers

IN THIS SECTION, I will provide some examples you may customize to fit your needs. The following poll samples might engage your audience and provide insights that can enhance your content strategy and strengthen your connection with readers.

1 — Reader Preferences for Content Depth

"When you read my articles, do you prefer quick tips, in-depth guides, or detailed case studies?"

Benefit: Understanding your audience's preferences helps tailor your writing style to meet their expectations, enhancing engagement.

2 — Post-Series Ideas

"What series would you find most valuable: Freelance budgeting tips, building a client base, or time management strategies?"

Benefit: Creating a series based on reader input generates anticipation and ensures your content aligns with their interests.

3 — Feedback on Recent Content

"How did you find my last article on XYZ topic? Did you love it, find it okay, or think it needed more details or other improvements?"

Benefit: Direct feedback allows you to refine your writing, improving future articles based on what resonates with your audience.

4 — Favorite Tools and Resources

"Which tools are essential for your freelance work: writing software, project management apps, or time tracking tools?"

Benefit: Gathering insights on preferred tools enables you to create valuable content that discusses these resources, establishing you as a trusted source.

5 — Success Stories and Challenges

"What was your biggest freelance win this month, this year, or in the last three years? You may give options such as "Did you land a new client, complete a challenging project, or achieve a personal goal?"

Benefit: Highlighting readers' successes encourages community and motivation, inspiring others and creating a supportive environment.

7 Best Practices for Using Polls to Get Optimal Outcomes

FROM MY RESEARCH EXPERIENCE, using the following best practices might help you maximize the effectiveness of polls and strengthen your connection with your audience.

1 — Design Clear Questions: Create concise, easy-to-understand poll questions that encourage thoughtful responses.

2 — Determine Optimal Frequency: Conduct polls every few weeks or months, depending on your content schedule and audience engagement. Too many polls might bore readers.

3 — Analyze and Act on Results: Analyze poll results to gain insights, inform your content strategy, and document them in your stories as references.

4 — Engage with Poll Respondents: Follow up on poll results by acknowledging reader input in your next newsletter or article, creating an engaging dialogue.

5 — Promote Poll Participation: Encourage readers to participate by highlighting the importance of their opinions and how they shape your content in the introduction section of your polls.

6 — Share Results: Transparently share poll results with your audience to cultivate a sense of community and encourage future participation.

7 — Test Timing: Experiment with the timing of your polls (e.g., after a specific article or at the end of a month) to find when your audience is most responsive. Unlike LinkedIn, the substack allows unlimited time for your polls.

How to Create an Online Poll in Substack Posts or Newsletters

IT IS VERY EASY TO create an online poll on Substack. When you have a draft document, you click on More and choose the poll option, as shown in the following screen capture.

It will create a framework like the following screenshot.

When you click on the edit button, which I highlighted above, you will get a frame in which you can populate your information.

Who can vote?

All subscribers who can see this post

Only paid subscribers

All subscribers who can see this post

Can we hide the number of voters?

YES, YOU HAVE THE OPTION to hide the number of votes, but I prefer to display them to increase my readers' confidence.

For example, if the number of votes is low and I make a statement, I include a caveat, noting that the sample size is limited, so the results may vary with a larger population. This adds an ethical layer to the interpretation.

Conclusions and Key Takeaways

AS A FREELANCE WRITER, understanding the purpose and benefits of polls and following best practices can gather valuable data, enhance meaningful engagement, and create a more connected community around your writing.

As I pointed out in the story, the Substack poll has limited features at this stage. So, you may consider third-party tools. For example, when I had a **dilemma with Facebook**[7] suspension, I used **the SurveyMonkey poll tool**[8] and gained valuable insights from my readers.

If you have used polls and benefited from them, please share your experience so that we can learn from each other.

Thank you for reading this chapter, providing feedback on the versions of this chapter you read, and also **participating in my online poll today.**[9]

Many writers ask why I emphasize the community aspect of platforms so much. The answer is simple: platforms like Substack can feel lonely and isolated without a strong community.

---

7.   https://medium.com/illumination/dilemma-should-i-trust-faulty-ai-to-restore-my-20-year-old-facebook-account-de5364c9e2ba

8.   https://www.surveymonkey.com/r/X9N5LJV

9.   https://drmehmetyildiz.substack.com/p/as-a-freelance-writer-which-writing

I learned this firsthand during my first six months on Medium, which was anything but enjoyable. Building a supportive community changed everything.

Besides, I have yet to encounter any successful writer, bestselling author, or leading Substack creator who thrives without being part of or leading a community. Community isn't just an add-on; it's essential for lasting success.

Chapter 18: Why and How to Add Surveys to Substack

Benefits of surveys and how to create them

In an earlier chapter, I discussed how polls can bring energy and interactivity to newsletters. While polls and surveys share some similarities, they differ significantly in scope and depth.

Polls are quick, providing a snapshot of opinion on a narrow topic. In contrast, surveys offer a broader, more detailed understanding, allowing us to dive into our readers' thoughts, preferences, and demographics.

Surveys, in particular, can be a powerful tool for uncovering valuable insights into who your readers are and what they expect from your content.

One of my key goals in using surveys is to gather demographic information — learning about the age, gender, location, and occupation of my audience. For example, if you write a finance blog and discover your readers are primarily young professionals, you might focus more on budgeting tips or career-related financial advice.

Content preference is another area where surveys shine. I have used them to gauge which types of content resonate most with my readers — whether it's news, tutorials, personal stories, or something else.

For instance, in a newsletter about technology trends, a survey could reveal that your readers are more interested in AI than cryptocurrency. This insight can help you adjust your content strategy accordingly.

In my health and wellness newsletter, I asked readers about their fitness goals — whether they were more focused on weight loss, strength training, or stress relief. Based on their responses, I was able to tailor future content to meet their needs, diving deeper into popular topics like weight loss strategies or stress management techniques. This approach not only enhances relevance but also strengthens reader loyalty.

Surveys also give readers a voice in shaping the content they receive, which can foster a greater sense of investment and belonging. By involving them in decisions — whether you're asking for input on the next series topic or seeking opinions on a new idea — readers feel like valued contributors rather than passive consumers.

For example, if you're planning a series on mental health, a survey asking which specific issues — anxiety, depression, or burnout — are most relevant to your audience will make them feel like their input matters.

Moreover, surveys can create space for open dialogue and community building. A Substack creator focused on political commentary might use a survey to ask readers for their views on upcoming elections or hot-button policy debates, sparking engagement and giving readers a sense that their opinions are not only heard but also shape the conversation.

Surveys are also a great way to gauge your audience's willingness to pay for certain types of content or premium subscriptions. You could ask them what kind of exclusive content — such as behind-the-scenes material, expert interviews, or early access to articles — would entice them to become paying subscribers. This can be instrumental in developing a monetization strategy based on actual demand.

I have used surveys to test new ideas as well. They allow you to float concepts to your audience before investing significant time or resources, offering immediate feedback on whether an idea resonates. This can save you from committing to projects that may not interest your readers.

Conducting regular surveys also helps track changes in your audience's preferences over time. This allows you to stay adaptable, continuously meeting their evolving needs. For example, if a lifestyle blog starts noticing a growing interest in sustainability, it can focus more on eco-friendly content to stay relevant.

If your Substack leads to product offerings like eBooks or paid content, surveys can help track changes in demand for various products or services. An educational Substack offering writing workshops might run quarterly surveys to gauge interest in different topics — such as fiction, non-fiction, or business writing.

If over time, they notice rising demand for business writing workshops, they can expand this offering accordingly, ensuring their content stays both fresh and aligned with their audience's desires.

In summary, surveys are a multifaceted tool that goes beyond data collection. They deepen reader engagement, help shape content, and offer crucial strategic insights to keep your Substack relevant and responsive. I will briefly guide how to start creating surveys on Substack.

Step-by-Step to Create a Survey on Substack

THE FOLLOWING SCREENSHOT I captured from my newsletter highlights the key points for creating a survey. I will provide a quick summary below.

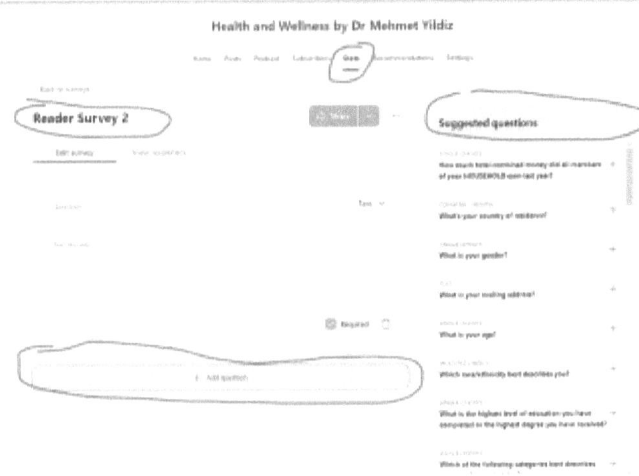

Step 1: Create a New Survey

1. Sign in to your Substack account.
2. Navigate to the Stats tab in the dashboard.
3. Click on Reader Surveys to open the survey creation tool:

THE FOLLOWING LINK will take you there:
https://your.substack.com/publish/stats/reader-surveys.
A pre-made survey titled "New reader survey" will appear.

Click Edit to modify this default survey.

If you want to start a new survey, click Create a new survey.

If you haven't edited the default welcome email templates, this new reader survey will automatically be included in the new subscribers' welcome emails.

To remove the survey link from these emails, edit the "Welcome email to free subscribers" and "Welcome email to paid subscribers" templates and delete the survey button.

Step 2: Edit the Survey

CHANGE THE SURVEY NAME:

Click on the three dots and choose Edit name.

Add and Customize Questions:

Click +Add question and select the type of question:

Text: Readers type their responses.

Number: Readers input a numerical response.

Multiple Choice: Readers select one or more answers.

Single Choice: Readers select only one option.

Country/Region: Readers select their country or region from a dropdown.

You can add possible responses or allow readers to input their answers by selecting Add Other.

To make a question mandatory, check the box next to Required.

You can use the up/down arrows next to the "Order" option to rearrange questions.

Step 3: Share the Survey with Subscribers

ONCE YOUR SURVEY IS ready:

1. Click Save Changes.
2. To share:

Click Share and choose either Send Ad-Hoc Email (this will not appear in your web post archive) or Copy a direct link to send via other platforms.

To embed the survey in a post, start a draft and select Buttons from the editor toolbar. Choose Link to survey from the dropdown, select your survey, and customize the button text.

Step 4: View or Export Survey Results

GO TO THE SURVEYS PAGE and click View Responses to see your survey **responses**.

To export responses as a .csv file, click the three dots next to the survey name and choose **Export results**. The export will include the subscriber's email address or Substack profile information.

Subscribers must be signed in to respond to surveys.

You will need to check responses manually — Substack doesn't notify you when new submissions come in.

This method allows you to engage your readers while gaining insights into their preferences and enhancing community interaction.

As these instructions might change in the future, it is a good idea to check **the official support page on Substack.** [1]

Takeaways

SURVEYS ARE MORE THAN just a tool. They are a bridge between you and your readers, transforming passive consumption into active participation. Using surveys can open more profound insights into your audience's demographics, preferences, and content expectations, helping you fine-tune your strategy to better serve their needs.

Surveys are great for gathering information. They create a two-way dialogue that boosts engagement, fosters loyalty, and strengthens the connection between your readers and your publication.

Moreover, tracking trends over time gives you a unique advantage in anticipating shifts in your audience's interests, allowing you to evolve your content in sync with their needs. This proactive approach can be crucial for maintaining relevance and driving long-term growth.

---

1.   https://support.substack.com/hc/en-us/articles/23659170380180-How-do-I-use-surveys-on-Substack

In addition to Substack's built-in surveys, you can integrate third-party tools like Google Forms, SurveyMonkey, or WordPress Forms. This opens up even more customization options, allowing you to craft tailored surveys that align perfectly with your publication's goals.

Whether testing new content ideas or exploring monetization opportunities, surveys provide a strategic, data-driven way to shape your Substack's future while keeping your readers invested and engaged. So, it is a good idea to add your surveys to your growth strategy on Substack.

Chapter 19: How Substack Writers Can Leverage Reedsy to Become Published Authors and Scale Their Publishing Business with Global Collaboration

This chapter promises to be an eye-opener for many freelance writers, as I have yet to come across a comprehensive guide on this tool across Substack, Medium, or other writing platforms.

In this advanced chapter, I am excited and delighted to bring this remarkable gem to light in 15 minutes, as it can be a game changer for established and aspiring authors. Reedsy is so comprehensive that it could require writing a long book. In fact, I have a comprehensive manuscript for my content marketing strategy clients, which I plan to publish as a guiding book with many case studies soon.

As a seasoned author with a track record of successfully publishing multiple books on different topics and working as a content strategist for freelance writers and content entrepreneurs, I have learned that high-quality content, compelling design, and strategic marketing are essential for growing audiences on any platform, including Substack.

Whether you aim to expand your Substack newsletters or transform your best articles or stories into books, identifying the right tools and professionals to support your journey is crucial. That is where Reedsy comes in, and I will give you a glimpse.

For those unfamiliar, Reedsy is an online marketplace designed for writers, giving you access to professional editors, designers, and marketers. But it doesn't stop there — Reedsy also offers self-publishing resources and tools to help you sharpen your skills. In this chapter, I shall explain how Reedsy can benefit you as a Substack writer and discuss its strengths and limitations in seven sections.

Purpose of This Advanced Chapter

WHILE I CRAFTED THIS chapter primarily for advanced writers and published authors, aspiring writers on Substack who are thinking about writing a book may also find it helpful.

My goal is to introduce another powerful tool for Substack writers to consider — one that you can embrace if it aligns with your needs and aspirations or set aside if it doesn't. I am simply a messenger and strategist offering you options to choose from.

In this chapter, I will profile a summary of the manuscript designed to onboard freelance writers and content entrepreneurs to Reedsy, highlighting compelling reasons for this and covering the pros and cons independently.

Please note that this is not sponsored content and does not represent Reedsy's official stance. They may have a different perspective, and I respect their position with gratitude. Instead, this chapter reflects my personal experiences and observations from my collaborators, students, colleagues, and protégés to provide you with a comprehensive, unbiased perspective.

How Substack Writers Can Leverage Reedsy to Become Published Authors and Scale Their Publishing Business with Global Collaboration

1. Professional Editing for Elevating Your Content

KEEPING YOUR CONTENT polished and error-free can be a real challenge for Substack writers. That is where Reedsy comes in. It connects you with professional editors — whether you need developmental editors, copy editors, or proofreaders — who can help refine your writing.

While Substack makes self-publishing a breeze, quality matters when it comes to building your credibility as a book author.

Having a Reedsy editor review your work means it is grammatically correct, engaging, memorable, and eye-catching. A good editor can help you communicate your message more clearly, which can lead to better reader retention and more subscribers.

Pros: You gain access to experienced editors who know the publishing industry. **Cons:** The costs can add up, especially for freelance writers who are just starting.

2. Branding and Design: Making Your Substack Stand Out

REEDSY ISN'T JUST ABOUT editing. It is also a fantastic resource for professional design services. Strong and memorable branding can set your Substack apart.

When you need a custom logo, newsletter headers, or eye-catching visual elements like infographics, Reedsy's designers can help you create a cohesive and appealing look for your newsletter.

Having a clean and visually engaging design helps you stand out and enhances the overall reader experience. Good design gets overlooked, but it is necessary for building a loyal audience.

Pros: Custom branding from professional designers can elevate your newsletter's visual appeal.

Cons: High-end design services can be pricey if you're on a budget.

3. Expert Marketing Guidance: Growing Your Readership

WHILE SUBSTACK PROVIDES basic tools for audience engagement, growing your readership often requires a strategic marketing plan. Reedsy's marketplace includes marketing professionals with publishing experience who can help you fine-tune your strategies for SEO, audience growth, and social media.

A Reedsy marketing expert can provide tailored advice to improve discoverability and engagement. This could result in more subscribers and a more dedicated readership.

Pros: Expert, personalized marketing guidance.

Cons: Marketing services can be expensive, and results may take time.

4. Learning Resources and Courses: Strengthening Your Writing and Marketing Skills

BEYOND HIRING PROFESSIONALS, Reedsy offers free and paid courses on writing, marketing, and self-publishing. These resources are perfect for Substack writers wanting to improve their skills or explore strategies to grow their newsletter.

If you are new to freelance writing and just started with Substack, Reedsy's courses can guide you on email marketing and content structure — both crucial for building a loyal following. These courses also help improve storytelling, which is key for keeping your readers engaged.

Pros: Self-paced courses to boost your expertise.

Cons: While some resources are free, more in-depth courses often come with a price tag.

5. Collaboration Opportunities: Expanding Your Content Offerings

REEDSY CAN BE A HUB for collaboration. Writers, designers, and editors working together can lead to new content ideas and joint projects that add value to your newsletter.

You might collaborate with a Reedsy designer to create infographics or e-books, adding visual appeal and increasing reader engagement. Collaborations like this can boost your subscriber rates.

Pros: Creative collaborations that enhance your content.

Cons: Managing collaborations can require extra time and resources.

6. Self-Publishing Your Substack Content and Turning Articles or Stories into Books

MANY SUBSTACK WRITERS dream of expanding beyond newsletters, perhaps by publishing an e-book or printed book. Reedsy offers a full suite of self-publishing services, from formatting to cover design and distribution, on platforms like Amazon, Kobo, Apple, or Google Books.

For instance, you could compile your best Substack articles into an e-book with Reedsy's help, giving your readers more value while opening a new revenue stream. I provided additional guidance to turn your stories into book chapters in an article. **Here's How to Create A 30,000 Words E-book in a Month and Start Earning.**[1] For example, **Aiden (Owner of Illumination Gaming)**[2], used this approach to write his first gaming book, for **which I wrote a forward.**[3]

Last year, editors also interviewed me and published the script in a story on this platform titled **How Writers and Bloggers Transition to Become Published Authors**[4]. Curators of my stories turned **the interview script into an interactive video**[5] and donated it to my Patreon library as a valuable resource for free members.

Link to the free source in my Patreon Library[6]

Pros: Streamlined process for turning Substack content into a published book.

Cons: Self-publishing can be costly, and success often depends on effective marketing.

---

1. https://medium.com/illumination-blog/how-to-create-a-30-000-words-e-book-in-a-month-16d3f2b5098f

2. https://medium.com/u/4a2ec49665f7

3. https://medium.com/illumination-book-chapters/an-inspiring-foreword-to-my-gaming-book-2c5fe685fb80

4. https://medium.com/illumination-curated/how-writers-and-bloggers-transition-to-become-published-authors-b65f92886a2e

5. https://www.patreon.com/posts/how-writers-can-112502140?utm_medium=clipboard_copy&utm_source=copyLink&utm_campaign=postshare_creator&utm_content=join_link

6. https://www.patreon.com/posts/how-writers-can-112502140?utm_medium=clipboard_copy&utm_source=copyLink&utm_campaign=postshare_creator&utm_content=join_link

7 — Leveraging Reedsy Discovery for Promotion

REEDSY DISCOVERY[7] is a specialized platform that helps authors showcase their work to a broader audience. It enables readers to discover new books and offers authors the opportunity to submit their books for reviews and promotion.

Reedsy Discovery can be an effective tool for authors seeking to market their books and gain an audience, particularly those looking for curated exposure and professional reviews. However, it is important to manage expectations, as success will depend on both the platform's reach and the reception your book receives.

Pros:

Increased visibility: your book can be featured in front of a dedicated audience of readers who are actively searching for new books.

Curated reviews: professional reviewers offer feedback, which can increase credibility and boost interest in your work.

Audience building: by being part of a well-curated collection, you have a greater chance of gaining loyal readers who are interested in your genre.

Cost-effective promotion: compared to some marketing services, reedsy discovery provides a relatively affordable means of gaining exposure.

Cons:

Not guaranteed acceptance: your book needs to pass a submission process, and not all submissions are guaranteed a feature.

Limited reach: while it can boost visibility, the audience is still relatively smaller compared to major platforms like Amazonor goodreads on which i have a community for book authors.[8]

Review dependence: the success of your book on the platform may depend heavily on the quality and impact of the reviews it receives.

The Costs of Using Reedsy for Book Authors from Substack

REEDSY DOESN'T CHARGE for signing up or browsing professionals, but hiring editors, designers, or marketers comes at a cost. I'd like to provide a breakdown to give you a high-level perspective with an additional reference from an experienced book author.

---

7. https://reedsy.com/discovery

8.   https://medium.com/illumination-book-chapters/join-us-on-goodreads-7ba0814ea4af

Professional Editing:
Developmental Editing: $0.02–$0.05 per word
Copyediting: $0.01–$0.03 per word
Proofreading: $0.007–$0.015 per word
Design and Branding:
Book Cover Design: $500–$1,500
Newsletter Branding: $200–$500
Marketing Services:
Marketing Plans: $500–$2,000
Self-Publishing:
Formatting and Layout: $500–$1,500

For freelance Substack writers, these costs can add up quickly. But if you're focused on building a high-quality, sustainable content business, investing in Reedsy services can pay off over time.

Additional Perspective:

Around this time last year, an experienced book author **Alison McBain**[9], wrote a comprehensive and eye-opening piece titled **Hidden Costs of Self-Publishing**[10]. You can gain additional insights from this boosted and exceptional story.

Free Alternatives to Reedsy

IF YOU ARE NOT READY to invest in Reedsy services, you may consider the following free or low-cost alternatives:

Editing: Tools like Grammarly and ProWritingAid offer free grammar and style checks. You may also consider Hemingway Editor to simplify your content.

Design: Canva can help you create basic branding elements.

Marketing: Substack's recommendation features and organic social media growth can be effective with the right strategies.

My editing and curation team also offer a new 3-tiered low-cost service including marketing **as documented on my website**[11]. **Mike Broadly,**

---

9.   https://medium.com/u/24377e97c643

10.   https://medium.com/illumination/hidden-costs-of-self-publishing-9ffab531b1a7

11.   https://digitalmehmet.com/illumination-substack-community-support/

DHSc[12], a founding member of my community articulated **the service in an editorial bulletin[13]**.

I also covered additional marketing and sales options for self-published authors a few years ago in a story titled **Here's How I Sold 1,000+ Books in a Month with Minimal Investment First Time.**[14]

Summary of Key Features of Reedsy

REEDSY SIMPLIFIES THE freelancer hiring process, enabling authors to manage their budgets and requirements effectively. Here is a summary of key features.

Marketplace: allows authors to hire editors, designers, marketers, and ghostwriters across various categories such as editing, design, marketing, and translation.

Writing tools: offers a free online book editor for writing and formatting, including collaboration features.

Learning resources: provides courses, webinars, and articles on writing, publishing, and marketing.

Book marketing: tools and advice to promote books and reach broader audiences.

Community: a space for authors to connect with peers and industry professionals.

Here are additional features:

Reedsy Discovery: curated reviews of indie books and a submission option for authors.

Reedsy blog: offers articles on writing topics.

Reedsy live: free access to past presentations and events.

Reedsy prompts: weekly writing contests with cash prizes.

Literary agent directory: a resource for authors seeking traditional publishing routes.

Conclusion and Key Takeaways for Established or Aspiring Book Authors

REEDSY CAN BE A STRATEGIC tool for established and aspiring book authors who write on Substack. However, Reedsy isn't a magic bullet for instant

---

12.   https://medium.com/u/c0e38065f854

13.   https://medium.com/illumination/the-strategic-move-illumination-communitys-commercial-arm-for-charitable-success-039d29a28f65

14.   https://medium.com/illumination-book-chapters/the-joy-of-selling-1-000-books-in-a-month-with-minimal-investment-13a24a6354c1

success. It is a powerful platform that can help you elevate your content, grow your audience, and even transition from Substack to book publishing.

The flexibility to choose only the services you need — editing, design, or marketing — makes Reedsy a valuable tool for scaling your Substack newsletters and achieving your long-term writing goals.

Ultimately, success on Substack requires consistent effort, experimentation, and smart use of tools like Reedsy or **Patreon, which I introduced in another chapter**[15]. By leveraging the platform's professional services, you can boost your capabilities and position yourself for sustainable growth and success in the content business.

I invite all freelance writers and content entrepreneurs to join my Patreon for free and benefit from the resources I provide and those curated by the volunteer editors and curators of my writing and reading community on multiple platforms.

Interestingly, **Reedsy**[16] once maintained an active presence on Medium, publishing stories until 2019. However, they seem to have ceased contributing, likely due to a lack of visibility and engagement. Their final post in 2019 received only two comments and a handful of claps.

In a platform with over a million paid readers, 50,000+ writers, and many book authors, even authoritative content from an organization supporting millions of published authors struggled to gain traction. I don't blame them. Medium, as it stands, is not conducive to this type of content thriving.

That's why I am now strategically publishing my work on more powerful platforms to gain more visibility — those that amplify my voice, reach a relevant audience, and distribute content without unnecessary censorship.

---

15.   https://medium.com/illumination-curated/why-integrating-substack-with-patreon-can-take-your-writing-to-another-level-bc205a9fcba0

16.   https://medium.com/u/f7aff4175741

Chapter 20: 14 Powerful Tools, Platforms, & Strategies to Elevate Your Substack Newsletters & Skyrocket Your Audience

In this chapter, I am pulling back the curtain on the essential tools that have helped me and countless others build content empires from the ground up. This long chapter is a much longer (500+ pages) summary of a book I wrote over the last two decades.

I will introduce you to the powerful tools and key strategies that simplify workflows, boost visibility, and engage audiences in ways that keep them coming back for more. If you have ever wondered how accomplished writers or best-selling Substack authors manage to create, promote, and profit from their content consistently, this chapter holds the answers.

Are you ready to turn your passion for writing into a thriving business with an audience that hangs on every word and a steady stream of income flowing in? It is not a dream. It is a reality for those who know how to use the right tools.

But let me tell you a secret: success in the content world isn't just about writing great pieces or having thousands of fake followers. It is about mastering the art, science, and technology of content creation in an ecosystem hosting your content — the behind-the-scenes machinery that propels your work to new heights.

Whether you are a freelance writer looking to scale your business or a content entrepreneur ready to break through the noise, these tools are the game-changers that can transform your journey. Ready to unlock your full potential? Let's dive into this special chapter to elevate your newsletters and skyrocket your audience.

Why I No Longer Provide Long-Form Content on Medium

I have reached a turning point as a creator on Medium. After pouring my heart into long-form content — deep, thoughtful pieces meant to provide real value — I have found that anything exceeding 10 minutes of reading time is overtly suppressed by the platform's algorithm.

Chapters of the bestselling Substack Mastery book stretching to 12 minutes or more received a soul-crushing ten views, at best from direct links. For a creator with 100K+ followers supporting 32K+ freelance writers through my 15 publications, this is devastating. It is more than discouraging. It feels like the platform itself is silencing in-depth work.

As I reflect on my journey over the past six months, I feel compelled to address the unspoken disconnect I have observed between Medium and Substack. My deepening commitment to Substack arose from a palpable sense of neglect from Medium (a platform I invested 5 years of my time) regarding my content. I want to highlight this intriguing dynamic, highlighting how it impacts authentic creators like myself and the potential for collaboration that seems to be overlooked.

It is perplexing, to say the least. The Medium algorithm appears to censor content related to Substack for reasons that remain shrouded in mystery, as evident in my statistics and observation of many writers contributing to my Substack Mastery and Curated Newsletter publication. This is not a speculation. I have enough empirical evidence to back up this claim. But it is not my focus anymore.

This baffling dynamic is particularly frustrating, considering that my book presents Substack as a collaborative platform, not a competitor. While Substack welcomes and embraces every piece I craft about Medium, my observations suggest that Medium has yet to return that generosity.

This lack of reciprocity raises questions about the true spirit of community within our creative ecosystems. As I navigate this landscape, I can't help but wonder: why not uplift one another instead of stifling potential collaborations? The future of content creation should be about unity, not division, and it's time to rethink our approach to these platforms.

As a result of my poignant findings, I have decided not to share my extended content on Medium. Instead, I am offering it for free on my website and Patreon, where I can truly connect with my audience without artificial limitations. Distilled versions will still be available on Substack, where quality isn't stifled by arbitrary algorithms. The freedom to provide meaningful content is what drives me, and I won't compromise that.

Summary of 14 Powerful Tools and Approaches to Elevate Your Newsletters and Skyrocket Your Audience

1 — Blogging on your Website or Guest Blogging

Blogging has been one of my most trusted allies since the early days of the internet. It's an invaluable tool for freelancers and content entrepreneurs eager to elevate their writing business. The beauty of blogging lies in its versatility; you can create both short and long-form content that drives traffic, engages readers, and establishes your authority in your niche.

Maintaining a dedicated blog alongside your Substack is a strategic move that can pay off significantly. By sharing in-depth articles, tutorials, or opinion pieces, you create a wealth of content that enriches your readers' experience and links back to your newsletter. This symbiotic relationship fosters a loyal readership while boosting your SEO, making it easier for new readers to discover you.

Additionally, blogging allows you to experiment with different writing styles and topics, honing your craft and identifying what resonates best with your audience. You can leverage your blog to delve deeper into subjects that may be too expansive for a newsletter format, providing value that keeps your readers coming back for more.

In essence, blogging is beyond a writing tool. It is a powerful mechanism for growth and connection. By integrating a blog with your Substack efforts, you position yourself as a thought leader in your field and lay the groundwork for a thriving writing career.

I have written extensively about blogging and guest blogging as essential tools for Substack writers because they open doors to new audiences. Guest blogging, in particular, enables you to tap into established communities, driving traffic back to your Substack and enhancing your visibility. Each post serves as a platform to showcase your expertise and direct readers to your newsletter, creating a ripple effect that amplifies your reach.

2 — Email Marketing Tools

While Substack excels in providing a straightforward platform for newsletters, integrating additional email marketing tools can amplify your reach and effectiveness. Platforms like **ConvertKit**,

Mailchimp, and **Beehive** are invaluable for enhancing your email marketing strategy.

These tools allow you to build and segment your email lists effectively, enabling you to target specific groups based on their interests or behaviours.

For instance, ConvertKit offers powerful automation features that let you create customized email sequences and landing pages, making it easier to nurture relationships with your audience. Mailchimp's robust analytics provide insights into engagement metrics, helping you understand how your subscribers interact with your content.

One of the standout benefits I have experienced is the impact of personalized welcome emails for new subscribers. Crafting tailored messages not only makes new readers feel valued but also sets a positive tone for future interactions. Additionally, segmenting your audience allows you to send targeted content that resonates with specific groups, increasing engagement and building a loyal readership.

Other tools, like ActiveCampaign and AWeber, also provide advanced features such as A/B testing for subject lines and content, ensuring you find the most effective ways to connect with your audience.

For those looking to sell products or services, these platforms often include features for creating sales funnels that guide subscribers from initial interest to purchase. This capability can be a game-changer for monetizing your newsletter.

Using these email marketing tools alongside your Substack can transform your newsletter from a simple email into a dynamic communication channel that fosters deeper connections with your audience and enhances your overall writing business.

3 — SEO (Search Engine Optimization) Tools

Optimizing your content for search engines is essential in today's digital landscape. Effective SEO can significantly improve your visibility, helping you attract organic traffic to your Substack newsletters. By identifying relevant keywords, analyzing competitors, and understanding search engine algorithms, you can ensure your content reaches a broader audience.

I use various SEO tools to enhance my articles, making them more discoverable. Here are some standout options:

Yoast SEO: This WordPress plugin is incredibly user-friendly and helps optimize your content as you write. It provides real-time feedback on readability, keyword usage, and overall SEO performance, ensuring that your articles are not only engaging but also optimized for search engines.

Ahrefs: Known for its extensive database, Ahrefs offers tools for keyword research, backlink analysis, and competitor insights. As a Substack writer, you can leverage Ahrefs to discover high-traffic keywords relevant to your niche and explore what strategies your competitors are using to rank higher.

Moz: Moz provides a comprehensive suite of SEO tools that help you track your site's performance, discover new keywords, and analyze your link profile. Its user-friendly interface makes it easy for writers to get insights on how to improve their search engine rankings.

SEMrush: This all-in-one tool is fantastic for keyword research, site audits, and content optimization. SEMrush's keyword magic tool can help you generate ideas based on what your audience is searching for, making it easier to create relevant and engaging content for your Substack.

Ubersuggest: This is a great budget-friendly option that provides keyword suggestions, domain insights, and content ideas based on trending topics. Ubersuggest helps you identify low-competition keywords that can improve your chances of ranking well.

Keyword Tool: This tool is excellent for generating keyword ideas based on various platforms like Google, YouTube, and even Instagram. By using the Keyword Tool, you can discover what terms your potential readers are using in their searches, guiding your content creation process.

Google Search Console: This free tool allows you to monitor how your site performs in Google search results. You can see which queries bring traffic to your newsletter, identify indexing issues, and understand how your content is ranked.

Answer The Public: This tool visualizes search questions and suggests topics based on what people are asking online. By incorporating these queries into your content, you can create articles that address the interests and concerns of your audience directly.

Using these tools, I've been able to enhance my content for SEO, which boosts my visibility and attracts organic traffic. The key is to integrate SEO strategies into your writing process seamlessly, ensuring your newsletters not only resonate with your readers but also rank well in search results.

4 — Affiliate Marketing Tools and Platforms

Monetizing content through affiliate marketing can provide a valuable income stream for content creators. By strategically including affiliate links in my Substack articles, I can recommend products or services that resonate with my audience, earning commissions while maintaining trust.

Numerous affiliate marketing platforms make this process seamless. **ClickBank**, **ShareASale**, and **Amazon Associates** are some of the most popular options. They provide access to a wide range of products and services to promote, along with tracking tools that help me monitor earnings and optimize performance.

For more targeted opportunities, **CJ Affiliate** (formerly Commission Junction) and **Rakuten Advertising** offer partnerships with well-established brands. **Awin** and **Impact** are also great platforms for connecting with niche-specific affiliates.

I dive deeper into affiliate marketing in my book titled **The Power of Digital Affiliate Marketing: How Authors Can Write More And Earn Passive Income**[1], which is available **in 16 different bookstores**[2], at half-price for free members of my Patreon **in PDF format,**[3] and all its chapters are free for paid members. It is also available via **Direct Purchase — Epub**[4]. I have also shared **its chapters on** [5]**Medium.com**[6], offering insights on how freelance writers can leverage these platforms and tools to create additional income streams.

5 — Social Media Management Tools

Managing multiple accounts and scheduling posts can often feel overwhelming, but social media management tools can significantly lighten that load.

---

1. https://books2read.com/u/m2R2jj

2. https://books2read.com/u/m2R2jj

3. https://www.patreon.com/drmehmetyildiz/shop/affiliate-marketing-for-freelance-386139?utm_medium=clipboard_copy&utm_source=copyLink&utm_campaign=productshare_fan&utm_content=join_link

4. https://illumination.digitalmehmet.com/products/d-igital-affiliate-marketing-for

5. https://medium.com/illumination-book-chapters/the-power-of-digital-affiliate-marketing-chapter-1-95968b0bf2e9

6. https://medium.com/

I rely on these platforms to streamline my promotional efforts for my Substack articles across various social media channels. By scheduling posts in advance, I can maintain a consistent presence without the daily hassle of manual updates, allowing me to focus more on creating compelling content.

Engaging with my audience becomes much easier with these tools. From a single dashboard, I can monitor interactions, respond to comments, and participate in conversations across different platforms. This interconnectedness helps me build relationships and foster a community around my writing, which is essential for growth.

Moreover, analyzing performance metrics is a game-changer. With tools like Buffer, Hootsuite, IFTTT, and DIRV, I gained insights into which types of content resonate most with my audience. By understanding engagement levels, shares, and click-through rates, I can tailor my future posts to align with my readers' interests. This data-driven approach not only maximizes my reach but also ensures that I'm delivering the content my audience craves.

Social media management tools are indispensable allies in my writing journey. They save me time, enhance my visibility, and empower me to engage with my audience meaningfully, making it easier to grow my Substack and connect with readers.

6 — Content Collaboration Tools

Collaborative writing has never been easier. The right tools can significantly enhance the creative process. These platforms streamline brainstorming sessions, allowing me to organize and develop ideas with others effortlessly. I create shared documents with peers to outline upcoming articles, making it easy to brainstorm topics, plot outlines, and gather diverse perspectives.

For feedback, I rely on tools like Notion and Google Docs, which enable real-time collaboration. Notion allows me to create detailed project boards and to-do lists while also sharing articles for feedback and comments. Google Docs or Google Sheets are my go-to for drafting content since its comment and suggestion features make it easy for beta readers to provide input directly on the document.

I also use Trello and Microsoft Teams, which are great for organizing workflows and managing collaborative projects. Trello's card system helps me visualize tasks and deadlines, keeping everyone aligned on progress. Microsoft Teams provides a central hub for communication, ensuring that discussions and files are easily accessible.

In addition, platforms like Airtable offer a unique blend of database functionality and collaboration, allowing me to track content ideas and their progress while collaborating with team members. This way, I can maintain a clear overview of what's being worked on, deadlines, and responsibilities.

Content collaboration tools are invaluable in my writing process. They enhance the quality of my work through collective input and foster a sense of community and shared purpose among fellow writers and contributors.

7 — Data Analytics Tools

Understanding your audience is critical to creating content that resonates. Analytics tools are essential for gaining those insights. They allow us to dive deep into audiencebehaviour, helping me see what content performs best and where I can improve. I always make it a point to analyze traffic sources, subscriber engagement metrics, and reader demographics to refine my content strategy and ensure I'm meeting my readers' needs.

In addition to SubstackStatistics, which provides valuable insights specific to my newsletter, I rely heavily on Google Analytics. It offers a comprehensive view of my website traffic, allowing me to track which articles drive the most visitors and how long they stay engaged with my content. The detailed reports on user behaviourhelp me identify trends and adjust my writing accordingly.

I have also started using tools like Clicky, which offers real-time analytics, allowing website owners to monitor visitor activity as it happens. This feature is useful for understanding immediate reactions to newly published articles or blog posts.

Another favorite of mine is Hotjar. It provides heatmaps and session recordings, giving us visual insights into how readers interact with our site. By seeing where they click and how they navigate, we can optimize our layout and content for better engagement.

For social media analytics, platforms like Hootsuite and Buffer provide metrics on how my promotional posts are performing. They track engagement rates, clicks, and shares, giving me a holistic view of how my content resonates across different platforms.

Finally, tools like Fathom Analytics are great for privacy-focused insights, giving us the essential data we need without compromising our readers' privacy.

In summary, these analytics tools are invaluable in shaping my content creation process. They empower us to make data-driven decisions, ensuring we connect with our audience effectively and consistently provide content that meets their needs.

8 — Networking Platforms and Online Communities

Building connections with fellow creators and industry professionals can open many doors in your writing journey. Networking platforms allow me to engage in meaningful conversations, share insights, and promote my Substack articles to a broader audience. It is about cultivating those valuable relationships that can lead to collaborations, guest posts, or mentorship opportunities.

Engaging with online communities has been a great way to share my work and receive constructive feedback. I actively participate in relevant subreddits, such as r/writing and r/content_marketing, where I share my articles and join discussions on topics that interest me. These interactions not only boost my exposure but also allow me to connect with like-minded individuals who share my passion for writing.

Slack and Discord are other favourites of mine, especially for their interactive and supportive communities. Slack offers professional networking opportunities. In addition **to my own Slack workspace with 24,000+ members from Medium**[7], I have joined channels focused on writing and content creation, where members share resources and job opportunities and support each other's work.

I am part of several servers dedicated to writing and content creation, where members share their work, provide critiques, and discuss industry trends. This real-time engagement fosters a sense of camaraderie and collaboration, which is invaluable.

I also leverage LinkedIn to connect with professionals in my field. It is a great platform for sharing industry insights, participating in discussions, and promoting my Substack articles to a more professional audience. I often post updates about my latest pieces and engage with comments to foster deeper connections.

I wrote an interesting chapter about LinkedIn, which has been the most productive and lucrative for me.

---

7. https://medium.com/illumination/7500-25-writers-miss-an-opportunity-by-not-joining-our-slack-workspace-c7751bb4c466

Facebook groups are fantastic for niche communities. I have joined several focused on writing, blogging, and newsletters, where I can share my work and tap into a wealth of knowledge from other members. These groups often have scheduled discussions or prompts, making it easier to connect and collaborate.

On X Premium[8] (formerly Twitter), I engage with creators and industry leaders through threads and hashtags relevant to my niche. The fast-paced nature of the platform allows me to stay updated on trends while promoting my content in real-time.

Quora Spaces[9] has also been instrumental in establishing my authority which also generates a bit of income. By answering questions related to my expertise and linking back to my articles when appropriate, I drive traffic and build credibility within the community. I also have **a Reddit community.**[10]

Leveraging these networking platforms and online communities has been crucial in expanding my reach and building meaningful relationships with my audience. The connections I've made have not only enriched my writing journey but have also opened doors to new opportunities.

9 — Membership and Donation Platforms

Creating a membership model allows me to generate recurring income while offering exclusive content to loyal subscribers. These platforms make it easy to reward supporters with perks like exclusive articles, behind-the-scenes content, or early access to new material.

---

8. https://medium.com/illumination/why-i-upgraded-to-x-premium-as-a-content-developer-curator-and-marketing-strategist-70a060d185c7

9. https://medium.com/illumination/you-can-earn-income-from-your-content-on-quora-with-the-same-or-less-effort-you-invest-in-medium-4e89a4805ff7

10. https://medium.com/illumination/do-you-want-to-increase-the-chance-of-your-stories-going-viral-on-the-internet-4c52e79e42a2

Substack has a built-in paid subscription model, enabling writers to monetize newsletters easily. As I covered in previous chapters, you can offer free and paid content, providing subscribers exclusive newsletters, Q&A sessions, and community access.

In addition, we can use **Patreon.** Known for its flexibility, Patreon allows creators to set up different membership tiers with varying perks like exclusive content, direct interaction, and private community access. It's ideal for creators looking to build a more structured membership program.

I wrote a full chapter on integrating Substack with Patreon.

In terms of donation tools, there are several free or membership-based ones. You can also use them as content creation, curation, and sharing tools. I will summarize them.

Buy Me a Coffee: This platform is incredibly simple to set up and allows fans to make one-time donations or set up recurring payments. It's perfect for creators who want a lightweight way to offer supporters bonus content or shout-outs without complex tiers.

Ko-fi: Similar to Buy Me a Coffee, Ko-fi lets creators receive one-time donations or monthly support. It also offers a shop feature where creators can sell digital products or commission-based work alongside their memberships. For example, **our Substack Mastery community**[11] created a Ko-Fi page to update our members who might donate to their efforts.

Memberful: If you're looking for a way to embed a membership program directly into your website, **Memberful** integrates seamlessly with platforms like WordPress, allowing creators to offer paid subscriptions without leaving their site.

10 — Content Repurposing Tools

---

11. https://ko-fi.com/illuminationsubstackmastery

Why recreate content from scratch when you can transform existing pieces into various formats? Content repurposing tools are essential for maximizing the value of your Substack articles and reaching wider audiences. By reimagining my content, I can engage with followers on different platforms and keep my message fresh and accessible.

Repurpose.io[12], which automates the distribution of my content across multiple platforms. This tool enables us to take our articles or Substack newsletters and convert them into audio files for podcasting or snippets for social media posts. Automation can save us time, allowing us to focus more on content creation rather than distribution.

Canva is also a game-changer for creating eye-catching infographics and social media graphics. I often use it to visually summarize key points from my articles. With its user-friendly design tools, I can craft stunning visuals that attract attention and drive traffic back to my Substack.

For audio content, **Anchor** allows writers to easily turn written content into podcasts. I can read my articles aloud or even invite guest speakers to discuss the topics, providing my audience with a different way to engage with my content. The platform's ease of use means I can publish episodes quickly and share them across various listening platforms.

If you're looking to convert blog posts into slideshows, **SlideShare** is an excellent option. I often take key takeaways from my Substack articles and create presentations that I can share with audiences interested in learning from my insights. This not only boosts my visibility but also positions me as an expert in my niche.

Zapier can help automate workflows between different apps, allowing me to streamline the repurposing of my content. For

---

12. **https://repurpose.io/**

example, I can set up zaps to automatically post a link to my Substack article on various social media platforms as soon as it goes live.

For video creation, **Lumen5** is a fantastic tool that helps writers turn articles into engaging videos. With its intuitive interface, we can easily input text, and it generates a video complete with visuals, music, and captions. This boosts engagement on platforms like YouTube and Instagram and caters to those who prefer consuming content through video.

In summary, leveraging these content repurposing tools helps me maximize the value of my existing content, expand my reach, and engage with a diverse audience across various platforms. It's a powerful strategy that keeps my content relevant and accessible, ensuring I make the most of every piece I create.

11 — Voice and Podcasting Platforms

Exploring alternative mediums like voice and podcasting can significantly broaden your audience and amplify your reach. Over the years, I noticed that starting a podcast allows freelance writers to delve deeper into topics from their Substack newsletters and opens up opportunities to interview experts, share personal insights, and engage with a completely different audience. It's an excellent way to diversify content and return new readers to your Substack.

Anchor by Spotify is one of the most user-friendly podcasting tools I use. It makes creating, recording, and distributing podcasts seamless. Whether I want to convert a written article into an audio format or create an entirely new episode, Anchor allows me to record directly from my phone or desktop and distribute it to platforms like Spotify, Apple Podcasts, and more.

For those looking for more robust features, **Podbean** offers advanced analytics and monetization options, which makes it easier to grow a professional podcast while tracking listener engagement. I've found Podbean especially helpful for understanding listenerbehaviour, which allows me to tailor my podcast episodes to better meet their interests.

Buzzsprout is another great platform that provides high-quality hosting services and helps optimize my podcasts for directories like iTunes and Spotify. With its easy-to-use interface, I can upload my episodes, get detailedstatistics, and even promote my show with custom embedded players on my Substack or blog.

In terms of recording and editing tools, **Audacity** has been helpful. It's a free, open-source platform that allows me to edit my podcast episodes with professional-level precision. Whether I need to cut background noise, splice in interviews, or add intro music, Audacity makes it easy to produce high-quality sound.

For mobile-first solutions, **Pocket Casts** is a fantastic app for both recording and discovering podcasts. It's one of my go-to platforms for managing podcast subscriptions, which helps me keep track of industry trends and stay inspired by other creators.

If you're looking to combine podcasting with transcription services, **Descript** is an all-in-one audio tool that not only allows me to edit my episodes but also transcribes them, creating dual formats for readers and listeners. This is especially useful for making my content accessible to a wider audience.

Podcast Addict and **Player FM** are popular podcast directories, and I submit my show for additional exposure. These platforms have large, engaged communities that often lead to organic growth as listeners discover your content through recommendations or curated lists.

By using these voice and podcasting platforms in my content strategy, I can repurpose my Substack newsletters into engaging audio episodes that attract listeners who might not have found my work through written content alone. It's a fantastic way to diversify our audience, build deeper connections, and keep our message dynamic across various formats.

12 — Video Creation and Graphic Design Tools

Visual content has become essential in capturing attention and boosting engagement. By integrating videos and high-quality visuals into our content strategy, we can enhance the appeal of Substack newsletters and increase interaction across social media platforms.

To create promotional videos for Substack content, some of my collaborators and proteges use **Animoto**, a user-friendly video-making tool that allows them to quickly turn their articles into dynamic video summaries. It is ideal for creating short, engaging videos that we can share across platforms like Twitter, Instagram, or LinkedIn. Animoto's templates make it easy to craft professional-looking videos even without advanced editing skills.

Another tool freelance writers can use is **Adobe Spark** (now Adobe Express), which is ideal for video creation and graphic design. With Adobe Spark, we can create animated videos, Instagram stories, and even promotional slideshows that align with the themes of my articles. It's an all-in-one tool that provides the flexibility to craft visuals that stand out, whether I'm summarizing key points or creating branded content.

Camtasia is a go-to software for more robust video editing. It allows us to produce longer, in-depth video content, making it easy to record screen tutorials or deep dives on topics covered in my Substack. Camtasia also offers advanced editing features, from adding annotations and transitions to creating voiceovers — perfect for when I want to share detailed insights with my audience.

When it comes to graphic design, **Canva** is indispensable. Whether I'm designing infographics to summarize my stories or creating banners for social media, Canva offers a vast range of templates and customization options. I use it to create visually appealing content that enhances the reader's experience and encourages social sharing, driving more traffic back to my Substack.

For creating more detailed and intricate designs, **Affinity Designer** is a useful alternative to Adobe Illustrator. It is particularly useful for creating professional-level vector graphics, whether I'm designing logos, illustrations, or complex infographics. I appreciate its versatility, especially when I want to add unique touches to my visuals.

Piktochart is a useful tool for designing infographics that simplify complex information. It is a great platform for visualizing data or breaking down the key takeaways from my articles in a format that's easily digestible and highly shareable on social platforms.

To create engaging motion graphics, **Lumen5** is one of myfavourites. Lumen5 allows me to transform my written content into captivating video stories. Its AI-driven platform analyzes my articles and automatically suggests video templates, saving me time while ensuring the visuals are on point. This is particularly effective for sharing bite-sized summaries or quotes from my Substack articles.

For photographers or creatives who want to include original images, **Adobe Lightroom** is an excellent tool for enhancing and editing photos. High-quality visuals can greatly enhance the professionalism of a blog post, and Lightroom offers comprehensive editing capabilities for those looking to incorporate stunning imagery into their articles.

Lastly, for simple and quick image creation, **Snappa** is a great tool for designing social media graphics, blog headers, and ads. It is an easy-to-use platform that allows me to whip up visuals on the go, particularly when I need something fast to accompany my Substack promotions.

By integrating these video creation and graphic design tools into my content workflow, I'm able to diversify the types of content I share and keep my audience engaged across different platforms. Visual storytelling, whether through videos, infographics, or custom graphics, complements my written work and enhances the overall reading experience while also helping my content stand out in a crowded digital landscape.

13 — Online Courses and Webinars

As a seasoned educator, I know that offering educational content is a powerful way to establish yourself as an authority in your niche while creating value for your audience.

By developing online courses and hosting webinars, I have been able to dive deeper into the topics I write about on Substack, offering a more interactive and engaging learning experience.

There are plenty of platforms available for creating and delivering courses, such as **Teachable**, **Udemy**, **Kajabi**, **Thinkific**, and **Podia**.

These platforms make it easy to build courses, manage students, and even integrate marketing tools to promote your content. You can also use **WordPress** with plugins like **LearnDash** or **WooCommerce** to create a fully customizable learning environment.

For live sessions and interactive webinars, tools like **Zoom** are essential for connecting with your audience in real time. Whether you're teaching a course or hosting a Q&As, webinars allow for a personal touch and open the door for immediate feedback and engagement.

Gathering feedback from your audience is essential for growth, and polls and surveys are great ways to directly engage with your readers. They allow me to understand my audience's interests and preferences, helping shape future content that resonates more deeply with them.

While Substack offers a built-in poll feature, it has its limitations. To overcome this, I often use more versatile tools like **Typeform** and **SurveyMonkey**, which offer advanced customization options, better data collection, and a more engaging experience for participants. These tools can easily be embedded into newsletters to reach your audience directly.

Other platforms like **Google Forms** and **Jotform** are also effective for creating simple surveys, and **Polldaddy** or **Crowdsignal** offers specific poll functionalities that can increase reader interaction in a more streamlined way.

14 — Content Calendars, Content Curation Tools, Collaborative Writing Platforms, Feedback and Editing Tools

Staying organized and producing quality content requires the right set of tools across several functions. Using the combination of tools I introduce below keeps my workflow smooth, my content high-quality, and my audience engaged.

Content Calendars: Organization is key for consistent publishing. I use tools like **Trello** and **Asana** to create detailed content calendars that track topics, deadlines, and promotion strategies. For more advanced options, tools like **CoSchedule** and **Notion** offer collaborative and visual planning features to keep everything aligned.

Content Curation: Sharing valuable content from others is just as important as creating your own. For curation, tools like **Pocket** and **Feedly** allow us to collect articles, blogs, and news to share with my audience in newsletters or on social media. Platforms like **Scoop.it**[13] and **Curata** help streamline this process, ensuring that I stay on top of the latest trends while positioning myself as a thought leader.

Collaborative Writing Platforms like Wattpad offers exposure to new audiences and collaboration opportunities. I publish excerpts of my work or collaborate with other writers, directing traffic back to my Substack for more in-depth content.

Feedback and Editing Tools: Polishing content for clarity and impact is crucial. I rely on **Grammarly** to catch grammar mistakes and stylistic issues, while **Hemingway Editor** helps ensure that my writing is concise and readable. **ProWritingAid** offers deeper reports on style and consistency, and **Google Docs** allows for seamless collaboration with editors and beta readers.

Conclusions and Takeaways

Mastering the art and science of content creation isn't just about writing — it is about strategically using the right tools to elevate every aspect of your process. These 14 tools and platforms are more than just accessories.

They are your competitive edge, each one playing a crucial role in expanding your reach, optimizing your workflow, and cultivating a deeply engaged, loyal audience. When they are combined, they can make a ripple effect.

When you use the power of these resources, you aren't just amplifying your visibility — you are creating a content ecosystem where your content can thrive. You will find yourself producing better quality content and building relationships that last. Think of these tools as investments in your writing future — unlocking opportunities for growth, passive income, and influence.

---

13. https://scoop.it/

So, the takeaway is clear: don't just create — create smart, with intent and precision. By strategically blending the right tools, you will be able to supercharge your Substack journey, setting yourself up for long-term success and even redefining what's possible for writers in this digital age. What is the future of your writing career? It is in your hands — armed with these powerful tools.

Chapter 21: Sustaining Your Newsletters for Long-Term Success & Evolving with Your Audience & Community Around Your Work in 8 Steps

This chapter is different from the previous ones. It reflects insights from my 40+ years of writing experience on different topics, various platforms, and different styles with their ups and downs. It is a short memoir that gives you valuable insights.

Some newer writers may assume everything was smooth for me as a leader of a large writing community on Medium and Substack, that my journey was all rainbows and roses. This is because I tend to write optimistically and constructively on Medium. But the truth is, I have faced countless setbacks, challenges, rejections, and harsh criticisms behind the scenes—just like anyone.

I don't allow those challenges to derail me, though. I use them as fuel for growth, for pushing forward. Yes, as humans, those moments stung for everyone. But how I chose to respond to them made the difference for me.

There will always be sour grapes or harsh critics — some of them extremely negative to put you down, some just wanting to sabotage the work of creative and authentic creators. But they are the minority. **It is human nature.**[1]

I learned to overcome these challenges methodically with patience. By keeping an open mind, accepting the learning process, practising tolerance, approaching events with optimism, and staying humble and authentic, I have learned to survive, thrive, and grow despite challenges.

---

1. https://medium.com/illumination/human-nature-the-painful-challenges-of-empowering-writers-to-build-a-resilient-community-e045c070fbdf?source=user_profile---------45--------------------

In this chapter, I will outline the fundamental life lessons I have absorbed through the turbulence without overwhelming you with too many details.

This chapter is not just about surviving the hardships but also about how those hardships refined my journey and made me more authentic and resilient in my writing, editing, content curation, and digital marketing, which can guide beginners.

This is the story behind the curtain. It is what I hope will inspire others to keep going, even when the path seems uncertain, freezing cold, or too difficult or sometimes unbearable to continue. 😔

I wrote this chapter without chasing perfection or seeking praise, letting my words flow raw and unfiltered. These are the true expressions from my heart, higher self, and spirit — unpolished and authentic.

I chose not to mask myself with constant strength, nor to embody a Pollyanna-like optimism or the cheerful façade we often see from celebrities on Instagram or TV.

Instead, I welcome the reality of vulnerability and honesty in my writing to pass along my tacit knowledge and hard-earned experience. I specifically chose vulnerability to show that not every moment is bright, and that is okay.

This chapter reflects the reality of my journey, full of ups and downs, and I hope it resonates with anyone who has ever felt the same.

1 — Understanding the Honeymoon Period Might End

Like anyone, I had my honeymoon phase and still have that excitement. However, the efforts I made, and the responsibilities I took, no longer kept me in that state.

Starting a Substack can be exhilarating for beginners—the rush of ideas, the thrill of those first subscribers, and the positive comments from the fans—but as with any creative pursuit, keeping that momentum alive over time is the true test.

After the initial excitement fades, the challenge becomes clear: How do you keep your Substack thriving in the long run?

I focused on my plan, the strategies, positive mindset, and adaptability required to sustain and grow my Substack newsletters. It is not just about engaging my audience but about evolving alongside them in a constantly shifting landscape.

2 — Finding Your Rhythm and Sticking to It

When it comes to long-term success, consistency is our best friend. Readers appreciate reliability. They want to know that they can count on you to deliver content on a regular basis.

But consistency doesn't just mean sticking to a schedule. It means maintaining a certain standard of quality and staying true to the voice and values that attracted your audience in the first place.

For me, finding a sustainable rhythm was crucial. I experimented with different posting frequencies, tried out various content formats, and listened to my audience's feedback.

Over time, I settled into a pattern that worked both for my readers and for me, as the initial phases were stressful. This balance allowed me to keep producing content without burning out and ensured that my readers always had something to look forward to.

That said, it is important to remain flexible. Life happens, priorities shift, and sometimes, we need to adjust our schedules and give ourselves a break to rejuvenate.

The key in these circumstances is to communicate with our audience — let them know if we are taking a break, changing our posting frequency, or experimenting with something new. Transparency builds trust, and our readers will appreciate being kept in the loop.

For example, Substack created a pause button to prevent burnout. You can find it in the settings' payment section.

3 — Adapting to Change and Evolving Our Content Development and Marketing Strategies

The digital landscape is always changing. Nothing stays the same! What works today might not work tomorrow.

To sustain our Substack newsletters over the long term, we need to be willing to adapt. This could mean tweaking our content development or marketing strategy, exploring new formats, or shifting our focus to meet the evolving interests of our audiences.

I have had to pivot several times during my writing journey. Sometimes it was in response to feedback, other times it was due to changes in the platform or broader trends in digital media.

But each time, I approached these changes as opportunities for growth rather than setbacks. By staying attuned to my audience's needs and being open to experimentation, I was able to keep my Substack newsletters fresh and relevant to my loyal readers.

One of the most significant shifts I made was using more interactive content. As my audience grew, so did their desire for deeper engagement and connection.

By evolving my content development and marketing strategies to include interactive and innovative elements, I sustained my readership and strengthened the community aspect of my Substack newsletters.

4 — Monetization Strategies by Balancing Income and Integrity

As your Substack matures, monetization becomes a key consideration. Whether you are offering paid newsletter subscriptions, launching educational courses, writing books, or securing sponsorships, the challenge lies in generating income without compromising the integrity of your content or alienating your audience.

For me, this balance was about being selective and transparent. I didn't want to overload my readers with ads or promotions, but I also recognized the need to make my Substack financially sustainable, as without monetization turned on, Substack did not allow my newsletters to grow.

After realizing this fact, I carefully considered each monetization opportunity by giving some content to paid readers, most of them free for new subscribers, and weighing the potential benefits against the impact on my audience's experience.

One strategy that worked well was offering tiered subscription options. This allowed me to provide value to paying subscribers while still maintaining a free tier for those who preferred not to pay.

I also experimented with limited-time offers, exclusive content, and personalized services to founding members through Patreon or my website to add value for my subscribers without overwhelming them with constant upselling.

Monetization isn't just about making money — it is about creating a sustainable model that allows you to continue producing high-quality content while respecting your audience's trust and loyalty.

By being thoughtful and strategic about your monetization efforts, you can achieve this balance and ensure the long-term success of your Substack.

5 — Dealing with Plateaus with Strategies for Reinvigoration

Every creator experiences plateaus — those periods when growth stalls, engagement dips, or inspiration wanes. These moments can be frustrating, but they are also a natural part of the creative process.

The key is to recognise those challenging moments for what they are: opportunities to reassess, recharge, and reinvigorate your freelance business whether you use Substack, Patreon, or other platforms like YouTube, Medium, NewsBreak, Fiverr, Vocal Media, or Hubpages.

When I hit a plateau, my first step was to take a step back and analyze what was happening, reviewing my statistics, my fitness status in my smartwatch, and the feedback I got from friends, colleagues, loved ones, or even loyal readers.

When I reached a plateau, I honestly asked myself: Was my content no longer resonating with my audience? Had I become too predictable? Was I neglecting engagement? By identifying the root cause, I was able to take targeted action to break through the plateau.

Sometimes, the solution was as simple as shaking things up — trying a new format, tackling a fresh topic, or collaborating with another creator.

Other times, it required a more in-depth approach, like revisiting my content strategy or investing time in audience research. Regardless of the approach, the key was to remain proactive and not let the plateau define my Substack's trajectory.

One of the most effective strategies I found was to reconnect with my "why" — the passion and purpose that drove me to start my Substack in the first place.

By revisiting my original goals and motivations, I was able to reignite my enthusiasm and bring fresh energy to my content when I hit a plateau. This not only helped me overcome the plateau but also deepened my connection with my audience.

6 — Embracing Feedback by Listening, Learning, and Evolving

Feedback is one of the most valuable tools we have as a creator on Substack, Patreon, Medium, or other platforms. Whether it is praise, criticism, or suggestions, our readers' input can provide invaluable insights into what is working and what is not.

Of course, not all feedback is easy to hear. There were times when I received criticism that stung or suggestions that didn't align with my vision.

But instead of dismissing this feedback, I took it as an opportunity to reflect and grow. Sometimes, it led to changes. Other times, it reinforced my commitment to my original approach. Either way, it helped me evolve as a creator and maintain a strong connection with my audience.

To truly benefit from feedback, we must approach it with an open mind and a willingness to learn and change. Although some creators are afraid of it, **I welcome negative feedback**[2] and have been using it in my business and personal development for decades.

Throughout my writing journey, I made it a point to actively seek feedback from my readers. I asked for their thoughts on new ideas, invited them to share their experiences, and paid close attention to their comments and questions. This made my readers feel heard and provided me with a wealth of information that helped me refine my content and marketing strategies.

7 — Looking Ahead for Future-Proofing Your Substack Newsletters

As you look to the future, it is important to think about how to future-proof your Substack. This means sustaining what you have built and positioning yourself to thrive in a rapidly changing digital landscape.

For me, future-proofing meant staying informed about industry trends, being open to new technologies, and continually investing in my skills as a writer, editor, content curator, and digital marketer. It also meant being adaptable — ready to pivot when necessary and willing to welcome change as an opportunity for growth.

One of the most effective ways I have found to future-proof my Substack newsletters is to focus on building strong, authentic relationships with my audience and the community around my work.

Platforms may change, and algorithms may shift, but loyal, engaged readers and the community are the most valuable assets we can have.

---

2.   https://medium.com/sensible-biohacking-transhumanism/negative-criticism-initially-stinks-but-later-it-smells-good-and-tastes-delicious-11d3c377e999

By continuing to prioritize my readers and invest in my community activities, I have been able to create Substack newsletters that are not only sustainable but also resilient to ongoing changes. Life is unpredictable, and we should accept and enjoy the ups and downs to maintain our sanity.

8 — The Legacy of Our Work with Impact and Influence

As you sustain your Substack newsletters over time, it is worth reflecting on the legacy you're building. What impact do you want to have? How do you want to just influence your loyal readers and build a broader community with new readers from different backgrounds?

For me, the legacy of my Substack newsletters is about more than just the number of subscribers. It is about the connections I have made, the conversations I have sparked, and the value I have provided to my readers and the community I established. It is about knowing that my work has made a difference, even in small ways, in the lives of those who have engaged with it.

Your Substack newsletters have the potential to be more than just a platform for your ideas. They can be a lasting source of inspiration, education, entertainment, and meaningful connections.

You can create Substack newsletters that leave a meaningful legacy by staying true to your values and principles, evolving with your audience and communities, and sustaining your passion for the work you create as a solo creator, freelance writer, or content entrepreneur.

Key Takeaways

TO CONCLUDE THIS CHAPTER, I want to emphasize how creating and curating content with intention and creativity is key to connecting with a broader audience.

This journey with ups and downs has taught me that success in writing isn't just about following trends — it is about crafting stories that resonate deeply and leave a lasting impact on our audience.

The evolving nature of platforms demands adaptability, which has driven me to refine my strategies continuously. We all need to be adaptable to survive and thrive.

By focusing on our values and principles, we can cultivate authentic engagement and build lasting relationships with readers who value high-quality, meaningful, informative, educational, entertaining, and inspiring content.

Many writers ask why I emphasize the community aspect of platforms so much. The answer is simple: without a strong community, platforms like Substack can feel lonely and isolated.

I learned this firsthand during my first six months on Medium, which was anything but enjoyable. Building a supportive community changed everything.

Besides, I have yet to encounter any successful writer, bestselling author, or leading Substack creator who thrives without being part of or leading a community. Community isn't just an add-on; it's essential for lasting success.

Conclusions: Your Substack Journey with Final Takeaways for Every Stage

As we bring this book to a close, it is time to reflect on the journey we have taken together—from the first steps of starting your Substack to strategies for sustaining it over the long haul. Whether you are just beginning, finding your rhythm, or looking to refine your approach, I designed these key takeaways to guide you to succeed at every stage.

For Beginners: Laying a Strong Foundation

☑ START WITH PASSION: Your enthusiasm for your topic is your greatest asset. Write about what excites you.

☑ Define Your Niche: Focus on a specific topic that you're knowledgeable about and that resonates with you.

☑ Know Your Audience: Understand who you're writing for and tailor your content to their needs and interests.

☑ Be Authentic: Authenticity builds trust. Be yourself and let your unique voice shine through.

☑ Set Clear Goals: Whether it's growing your audience or improving your writing, know what you want to achieve.

☑ Consistency Matters: Develop a posting schedule you can maintain—consistency builds credibility.

☑ Experiment Early: Don't be afraid to try different formats and topics to see what resonates with your audience.

☑ Focus on Quality: Prioritize clarity, relevance, and engagement in everything you write.

☑ Engage with Readers: Respond to comments and feedback to build a loyal community.

☑ Learn from Others: Follow successful Substacks and learn from their strategies and techniques.

For Intermediate Writers: Building Momentum

☑ REFINE YOUR VOICE: As you grow, continue to hone your writing style and tone.

☑ Expand Your Topics: Gradually introduce new topics to keep your content fresh and engaging.

☑ Analyze Performance: Use analytics to understand what's working and where you can improve.

☑ Engage More Deeply: Consider adding interactive elements like polls or Q&As to increase reader engagement.

☑ Network with Other Writers: Collaborations and guest posts can help you reach new audiences.

☑ Monetize Thoughtfully: If you're ready to monetize, start with simple strategies like paid subscriptions or one-off contributions.

☑ Create a Content Calendar: Plan your content to stay organized and consistent.

☑ Diversify Content Formats: Mix things up with newsletters, essays, podcasts, or videos.

☑ Use Reader Feedback: Regularly ask for and incorporate reader feedback to improve your content.

☑ Stay Informed: Keep up with industry trends to ensure your content remains relevant.

For Advanced Writers: Scaling and Sustaining Success

☑ OPTIMIZE FOR GROWTH: Focus on strategies that scale, like referral programs or partnerships.

☑ Explore Advanced Monetization: Consider premium content, courses, or sponsored posts.

☑ Strengthen Community Ties: Foster a strong sense of community with regular engagement and exclusive perks.

☑ Diversify Revenue Streams: Don't rely on one income source; explore multiple avenues like ads, subscriptions, and merchandise.

☑ Invest in Professional Tools: Upgrade to tools that enhance your workflow, such as advanced analytics or email marketing platforms.

☑ Build a Brand: Think of your Substack as a brand, and ensure consistency across all touchpoints.

☑ Automate Where Possible: Use automation tools to handle routine tasks, freeing up time for creativity.

☑ Offer Personalized Content: Consider segmenting your audience to provide more tailored content.

☑ Host Events or Webinars: Engage your audience with live events to deepen relationships and offer value.

☑ Plan for Longevity: Think long-term—how will your Substack evolve in the next few years?

100 Key Takeaways for Every Stage of Building Your Substack

I categorized and created this checklist based on feedback from beta readers. The order might not reflect the importance you have in mind. The key point is considering the relevant points for your needs and discarding the irrelevant. My goal is to give a broad audience as many options as possible.

1. Foundation and Mindset

☑ **Passion Fuels Success**: Write about what you love.
  ☑ **Set Clear Goals**: Know what you want to achieve.
  ☑ **Define Your Audience Early**: Know who you're writing for.
  ☑ **Focus on Value**: Always provide value to your readers.
  ☑ **Quality Over Quantity**: Always prioritize content quality.
  ☑ **Authenticity Wins**: Be genuine in your writing.
  ☑ **Be Transparent**: Honesty builds trust with your audience.
  ☑ **Stay True to Your Voice**: Don't lose your unique voice.
  ☑ **Be Proud of Your Progress**: Acknowledge how far you've come.

2. Building Trust and Engagement

☑ **Consistency Builds Trust**: Stick to a regular posting schedule.
  ☑ **Engagement is Key**: Interact with your readers regularly.
  ☑ **Respond to Feedback**: Take reader feedback seriously.
  ☑ **Build a Community**: Foster a sense of belonging among your readers.
  ☑ **Share Your Story**: Personal stories help build connections.
  ☑ **Stay Humble**: Remember, there's always room for improvement.
  ☑ **Practice Gratitude**: Thank your readers for their support.

3. Growth and Adaptability

☑ **Be Patient**: Growth takes time.
- ☑ **Be Persistent**: Don't give up during tough times.
- ☑ **Don't Be Afraid to Pivot**: Adjust your strategy when necessary.
- ☑ **Test and Learn**: Experiment and refine your approach.
- ☑ **Be Open to Change**: Adapt to the evolving landscape.
- ☑ **Learn from Mistakes**: Analyze failures and learn from them.
- ☑ **Experiment to Grow**: Try new formats and topics.
- ☑ **Stay Informed**: Keep up with trends in your niche.
- ☑ **Be Adaptable**: Be ready to change your approach as needed.
- ☑ **Embrace Challenges**: View obstacles as opportunities for growth.

4. Strategy and Planning

☑ **Start Small, Think Big**: Focus on quality before quantity.
- ☑ **Track Your Progress**: Use analytics to guide your strategy.
- ☑ **Use a Content Calendar**: Plan your content ahead of time.
- ☑ **Refine Your Content Strategy**: Continually improve your approach.
- ☑ **Optimize Your Workflow**: Streamline your processes.
- ☑ **Set Realistic Goals**: Set achievable and measurable goals.
- ☑ **Think Long-Term**: Plan for sustained success.
- ☑ **Be Inclusive**: Welcome diverse voices and perspectives.

- ☑ **Maintain Boundaries**: Set healthy boundaries between your work and personal life.

5. Monetization and Scaling

- ☑ **Monetize Gradually**: Start with simple monetization methods.
- ☑ **Balance Free and Paid Content**: Offer both to cater to different audience segments.
- ☑ **Experiment with Monetization**: Test different revenue models.
- ☑ **Diversify Your Income Streams**: Don't rely on just one source of revenue.
- ☑ **Plan for Scalability**: As you grow, plan for a larger audience.
- ☑ **Offer Discounts**: Provide incentives to attract new subscribers.

6. Tools and Optimization

- ☑ **Use Analytics Wisely**: Understand what works and what doesn't.
- ☑ **Leverage Social Media**: Use social platforms to promote your Substack.

☑ **Utilize Analytics Tools**: Use tools to gain insights into your audience's behaviour.

☑ **Invest in Tools**: Upgrade your tools as you grow.

☑ **Invest in a Good Design**: A clean and professional look makes a big difference.

☑ **Focus on Deliverability**: Ensure your emails reach your subscribers.

☑ **Optimize for SEO**: Optimize your posts for search engines.

☑ **Offer Value in Emails**: Make your newsletters worth opening.

☑ **Keep an Eye on Competitors**: Learn from what others are doing.

☑ **Monitor Trends**: Stay updated with industry trends and adapt accordingly.

☑ **Stay Organized**: Keep your content and schedule well-organized.

7. Content Creation and Delivery

☑ **Offer Solutions**: Provide answers to your audience's questions.
  ☑ **Create Evergreen Content**: Write posts that remain relevant over time.
  ☑ **Diversify Content**: Mix up your content formats.
  ☑ **Create Value-Driven Content**: Always aim to provide value in every post.
  ☑ **Keep it Simple**: Don't overcomplicate your content or strategy.
  ☑ **Offer Exclusives**: Provide exclusive content for loyal readers.
  ☑ **Use Visuals**: Enhance your content with images and infographics.
  ☑ **Host Guest Writers**: Invite others to contribute to your Substack.
  ☑ **Provide Clear Calls to Action**: Guide your readers on what to do next.
  ☑ **Create a Content Library**: Build a collection of your best work.
  ☑ **Offer Limited-Time Content**: Create urgency with time-sensitive content.

8. Reader Experience and Interaction

☑ **Prioritize Reader Experience**: Make your Substack enjoyable to read.

☑ **Respect Your Audience's Time**: Keep your posts concise and to the point.

☑ **Personalize Your Content**: Make your readers feel special with personalized messages.

☑ **Be Clear in Your Communication**: Ensure your messages are easy to understand.

☑ **Listen to Your Audience**: Understand their needs and desires.

☑ **Run Surveys**: Understand your audience's preferences with surveys.

☑ **Ask for Feedback**: Regularly seek out reader opinions.

☑ **Leverage User-Generated Content**: Encourage your audience to contribute.

☑ **Host Webinars**: Engage your audience with live content.

☑ **Engage on Social Media**: Use social platforms to interact with your readers.

9. Inspiration and Growth Mindset

☑ **Stay Inspired**: Keep your passion alive.

☑ **Learn from Others**: Study successful Substacks.

☑ **Keep Learning**: Always seek to learn new skills and strategies.

☑ **Invest in Your Skills**: Continuously improve your writing and editing skills.

☑ **Think Beyond Writing**: Explore podcasts, videos, and other formats.

☑ **Celebrate Milestones**: Acknowledge and celebrate your achievements.

☑ **Be Open to Criticism**: Use criticism to improve your content.

☑ **Stay Consistent with Tone**: Keep your tone of voice consistent across all posts.

☑ **Stay Focused**: Don't get distracted by trends that don't align with your goals.

☑ **Create a Safe Space**: Foster a respectful and inclusive community.

☑ **Be Authentic in Promotions**: Promote your Substack honestly and transparently.

☑ **Invest in Your Growth**: Continuously seek ways to improve your Substack.

NOW THAT YOU HAVE REACHED the end of this guide, you are equipped with strategies, tactics, and valuable insights from my experience and observations that will help you at every stage of your freelance writing journey. Keep pushing forward, continue learning, and most importantly—keep writing! Your audience is waiting.

As this is the first version of the book, I will continue to update it with feedback from loyal readers like you. Please consider leaving honest feedback on the bookstore where you purchased this book. Thank you for your time for reading. I wish you and your loved ones the best. You can contact me via my website, Digitalmehmet.com, which has a contact link in the menu.

Best Regards,

Dr Mehmet Yildiz, Digitalmehmet.com, October 2024

ABOUT THE AUTHOR

Dr Mehmet Yildiz is a researcher and a technologist who worked as a Distinguished Enterprise Architect certified by the Open Group in multi-billion projects. Working in the IT industry over the last 42 years, leading complex enterprise projects for large corporate organizations like IBM, Siemens, and Microsoft, he focuses on cutting-edge technology solutions, such as IoT, Big Data Analytics, Blockchain, Cognitive Computing, AI, Cloud, Fog, and Edge Computing integration.

He is a seasoned writer and the author of multiple books on technology, health, science, and content development, combining decades of experience in science, technology, enterprise architecture, and corporate business leadership. With an academic, research, innovation, and invention background, Dr. Yildiz has made significant contributions to content creation, marketing, strategy, and digital innovation.

As the chief editor and owner of 15 prominent publications on Medium, he has built a thriving community of over 32,000 writers, supporting them in their creative journeys. His expertise extends to Substack, where he continues to cultivate a large, engaged community, guiding writers to discover their unique voices, grow their audiences, and develop sustainable newsletter-based businesses. Owning three newsletters on Substack, he gained over 28,000 subscribers. In his recent book Substack Mastery, Dr. Yildiz distills decades of knowledge into actionable insights, offering writers practical strategies to succeed in today's competitive digital landscape.

You can connect with the author on several platforms linked to his website digitalmehmet.com

| Page

About the Author

Dr Mehmet Yildiz is a technologist who worked as a Distinguished Enterprise Architect certified by the Open Group in multi-billion projects. Working in the IT industry over the last 42 years, leading complex enterprise projects for large corporate organizations like IBM, Siemens, and Microsoft, he focuses on cutting-edge technology solutions, such as IoT, Big Data Analytics, Blockchain, Cognitive Computing, AI, Cloud, Fog, and Edge Computing integration.

He is a seasoned writer and the author of multiple books on technology, health, science, and content development, combining decades of experience in science, technology, enterprise architecture, and corporate business leadership. With an academic, research, innovation, and invention background, Dr. Yildiz has made significant contributions to content creation, marketing, strategy, and digital innovation.

As the chief editor and owner of 15 prominent publications on Medium, he has built a thriving community of over 32,000 writers, supporting them in their creative journeys. His expertise extends to Substack, where he continues to cultivate a large, engaged community, guiding writers to discover their unique voices, grow their audiences, and develop sustainable newsletter-based businesses. Owning three newsletters on Substack, he gained over 28,000 subscribers. In his recent book Substack Mastery, Dr. Yildiz distills decades of knowledge into actionable insights, offering writers practical strategies to succeed in today's competitive digital landscape.

You can connect with the author on several platforms linked to his website digitalmehmet.com

Read more at https://digitalmehmet.com.